Waist Deep in Montana's Lakes

John Holt

WAIST DEEP IN MON- TANA'S LAKES

PRUETT PUBLISHING COMPANY
BOULDER, COLORADO

Printed in the United States
10 9 8 7 6 5 4 3 2 1

Library of Congress Cataloging-in-Publication Data

Holt, John, 1951–
    Waist deep in Montana's lakes / John Holt.
        p.   cm.
    Includes bibliographical references and index.
    ISBN 0-87108-822-3 — ISBN 0-87108-824-X (pbk.)
    1. Fly fishing—Montana. 2. Fishing—Montana. I. Title.
SH456.H62   1992
799.1'1'09786—dc20   92-12997
                                                              CIP

Some of the material in this book originally appeared in different form in
the following publications: *American Angler, Fly Fisherman, Flyfishing, Fly
Rod & Reel,* and *Petersen's Fishing.*

Permission to reprint a portion of *Blood Sport* generously granted by
Robert F. Jones. Copyright ©1974 by Robert F. Jones.

Permission to reprint a portion of *Stillwater Trout* generously granted by
Lyons and Burford, Publishers, New York, New York. Copyright ©1977
by Del Canty.

For Mom and Ken

My madness was total: sublime, ecstatic, unmarred by any doubts or sulks. At no point during the months I roamed that mean, lean country, killing for food and pleasure, do I recall one moment of reason, one instant of unhappiness. It was as if a caldron of liquid laughter had come to a slow, steady boil behind my eyes, perking joyfully there, sending shots of giggly steam down my nostrils and up my throat, exploding from time to time in scalding, superheated guffaws that left my vocal cords raw and aching with delight. I felt no fear, no hunger, no worry—only the immense, ridiculous power of my freedom.

Robert F. Jones, *Blood Sport*

Contents

Acknowledgments

Thanks go to Tom Weaver, Jim Vashro, and others at the Montana Department of Fish, Wildlife and Parks; Tom Rosenbauer and Doug Truax of the Orvis Company; Ken Menard of Umpqua Feather Merchants; Tony Acerrano for well-directed criticism; Jim Pruett for support and phone availability; and my wife, Lynda, for extreme patience.

Introduction:
Lost in the Ozone, Again

Mud coats the windshield an inch thick. The wipers strain to clear a line of sight through the chipped and scratched glass as the truck lurches and slides sideways, back and forth, to and fro, across the surface of a road turned greasy slop. Huge road-graders and haulers tower above as they pass, bound somewhere in the opposite direction.

The last time I was in this country the road surface afforded smooth sailing, an eighty-mile-per-hour cruise in search of coulee-and-bluff isolation. Not this time. The highway is torn up, and if I'm not careful, the same thing will happen to me.

This driving stopped being fun the minute the truck flew off the end of the paved portion of the highway heading east and south toward a reservoir in an isolated corner of Montana. Landing in the mud-under-construction was a shock, and the driving is tense, tough. Just maintaining forward momentum means driving faster than rational behavior suggests. A sign a while back said there were eleven miles of this ripped-up madness left, and really—what for?

The road has been a beaten-to-death metaphor for decades, and literary artifice has absolutely no place in this trip (or this book) except as a means to an end—in this case running down rumors of all sorts of exotic gamefish in a little-known piece of water in the heart of coal country.

There are turkeys in abundance in this land too, but the hunting is now on hold because of a spring storm that dumped two feet of snow on the ponderosa pine hills and wandering valleys. Moving off the main drag means getting stuck, probably for a long time. Not many people live out here, and those that do are smart enough to avoid travel in these sticky conditions. I am six hundred miles from home and have no choice in the matter. Trapped here or thirty miles up the road—what difference does it make? I am in all the way now.

Last year was devoted to fishing the rivers of Montana, and I would certainly spend many hours doing the same this season, but there are thousands of lakes in the state and I wanted to check out several that are shrouded in strange rumor. There are also a few that no one I spoke with knew anything about, and these I really want to fish. Unknown water in Montana? Hard to believe, but these types of things are always worth a gamble.

"You bet. There's a lake in those hills up by the border that has rainbow as thick as a round of Milwaukee bologna," said a guy in Connolly's Bar in Cut Bank, up along the Hi-Line. I am from southern Wisconsin, so I knew the dimensions he was describing, and this made me excited. "Damn easy to catch too, as long as you don't use any of that dinky fly-fishing shit. Another." And a finger pointed to a highball glass that was swiftly filled to the brim with bar whiskey.

I was in a hurry to get somewhere at the time, so I didn't have a chance to check out the story. This year I would, along with tales about places on Fort Peck Reservoir, the Tongue way over southeast, some unnamed lakes near my home in Whitefish, not far from Glacier Park, and a few others.

Trying to fish every piece of water in Montana is an absurd impossibility. Still, I like to check out at least a dozen new places each year. Variety, mystery, adventure, and all that jazz.

Still water is such a strange environment, especially after you've keyed to the varying rhythms of rivers and streams. Lakes, ponds, and reservoirs hold a subtle, softly defined attraction for me. On a calm day when the fish are not working the water looks like a desert—empty, without life or interest. Yet I know that just below the surface big fish are cruising and feeding. The challenge is to find them and their holding areas, and to divine what they are taking. Variety and mystery.

Del Canty describes a taste of this magic in *Stillwater Trout:* "The storm was picking up and it was getting windy. More fish started showing up. They really like that oxygen in the whitecaps. I cast to a couple of fish, but the wind was blowing me around so I couldn't get to them accurately. Then there he was. Right in the waves. I could see the whole fish. I was lucky; the fly fell right in front of his face. He turned a few inches and had the fly before I had really recovered. I hit the fish three times to set the hook."

That is lake fishing in its essence, and so is casting to dozens of rising cutthroats on a high mountain lake or flinging large streamers to marauding northerns in a shallow-water bay or working leech patterns in front of aggressive largemouths in reservoirs.

To sample some of this is the casual plan for the season that has its beginnings in this April mud and snow and will die a reluctant death somewhere in November, probably in a hailstorm that knocks a leaping rainbow senseless.

Such is life. Onward and upward. And as Fleetwood Mac used to say twenty years back, "Then play on . . ."

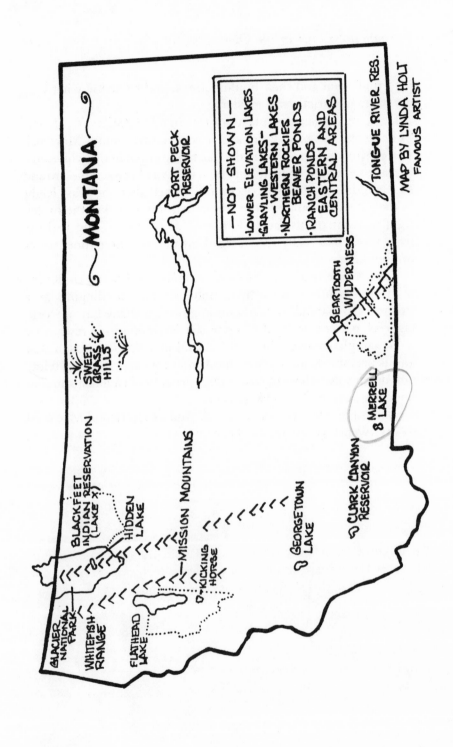

MONTANA

GLACIER NATIONAL PARK

WHITEFISH RANGE

FLATHEAD LAKE

BLACKFEET INDIAN RESERVATION (LAKE "X")

HIDDEN LAKE

MISSION MOUNTAINS

KICKING HORSE

GEORGETOWN LAKE

CLARK CANYON RESERVOIR

8 MERRELL LAKE

SWEET GRASS HILLS

FORT PECK RESERVOIR

— NOT SHOWN —
• LOWER ELEVATION LAKES
• GRAYLING LAKES — WESTERN LAKES
• NORTHERN ROCKIES BEAVER PONDS
• RANCH PONDS EASTERN AND CENTRAL AREAS

BEARTOOTH WILDERNESS

TONGUE RIVER RES.

MAP BY LYNDA HOLT
FAMOUS ARTIST

Tongue River Reservoir

*T*here was not anything to see around here anymore except wet, driving, blinding snow slicing down out of a swirling gray northwest sky and into my hurting eyes.

The van was not going anywhere on this little muddy rut wandering through the emptiness of far southeastern Montana. The front tires, even with chains, spun uselessly in a mud-gumbo amalgam that used to be red-brown dirt and dust in yesterday's clear sky and mid-eighties sunshine. Its momentum exhausted, the van slid back down the slight hill a few feet before coming to a greasy stop just barely on the road, for the moment.

Off the road meant that my friend and I would be seriously stuck and facing a world-class towing bill, that is, if we managed to walk out to anyplace with walls, electricity, and warmth. On the Custer National Forest map the distance looked to be five or six miles, but the information was last checked a decade ago, so who knows? The very small town of Ashland along the Tongue River was out there about twenty miles, which was probably out of our reach in this snow that was covering the ground at a steady couple-of-inches-an-hour clip. As for the Tongue River Reservoir where we'd fished yesterday, that was more like forty miles distant—another planet.

I climbed back into the damp warmth of the van. For a first turkey hunt and early-spring fishing outing, this was proving eventful.

1

Up until last September there was no way in hell I was going to hunt a turkey—not Down South, not Back East, and definitely not in the emptiness that is eastern Montana. I had enough problems without dressing from head to toe in camouflage clothing and makeup.

This all changed last September, when my companion, Steve, regaled me with tales of his adventures around here the previous spring.

"You had to be there John," (I'd heard this one before, and it usually meant trouble of some sort) said Steve with a wicked grin that was a little bit famous in certain parts of the state. "I was sitting down in this big clump of bushes and turkeys were gobbling everywhere. I'd call and two of them answered and they kept getting closer."

I could tell by the shine in his eyes that he knew I was hooked.

"I didn't move and these guys kept coming in on each side of me. Their heads were stretching up and looking around and I'd hear *gobble gobble gobble.* It was great. I had to shoot out of self-defense. They were in love. What could I do and think about all of those northerns and smallmouths and giant goldfish in the Tongue?" And all this told during a long trudge through the heat and dust of the badlands an hour east of the Little Bighorn, where Custer lost a fight over a century ago. At the time we were hunting sharptails and had not seen any, but would near evening. When you've been walking this long, next to a cold beer, any tale of believable madness is a welcome escape from the drudgery that is often part of my bird hunting.

"So, John. Do you want to go next year?" and Steve was really grinning now and I said "Yes," and I knew better. This was the guy who'd managed to coerce me into hunting sapphires and garnets along the Missouri River, moss agates on a partially sub-merged gravel bar in the middle of the Yellowstone River during spring runoff, brown trout on the Madison on one dead-of-winter October day, and northern pike hunting where our guides managed to get all three of their trucks stuck in the Flathead River.

These were the best of times, but we'd been lucky so far and

Early April: The Tongue Reservoir in all its starkness.

it was still early. And I knew Steve was right about the turkeys. Several flocks of over fifty birds each had silently drifted off into the ponderosa pine forest as we drove along gravel roads to and from our day's sharptail hunting. And he assured me that since few hunted the region, the birds were not exceptionally spooky, so I would not have to go "full-bore camo."

As for the Tongue River Reservoir, this scenic piece of water lay out in windswept coal country. Any time you stepped out of your car and listened around here, you could hear the gut-level rumblings of gigantic draglines and scoops and also that of trucks the size of the White House. This land was being blasted, dug, and pounded into big-business submission. Fortunately, for now at least, there was still plenty of the unspoiled variety left.

The pond was perhaps five miles long by a half-mile wide. Low rolling hills surrounded the shallow impoundment. In addition to the northerns and smallmouths, there were reported to be (by a somewhat reliable individual who operated the fly shop in

Whitefish) large goldfish that had been dumped into the reservoir by residents of the town of Sheridan, Wyoming, which was just five miles across the border to the south. There were also those truly sporting gamefish—walleye and sauger—eagerly waiting the attentions of those who enjoyed trolling license plates that were connected to minnows impaled on hooks. A fine pursuit, ranking right up there with hosting a thirty-minute TV show pitching hair-restorer. There were also some crappies and catfish drifting around in the slightly turbid water. And in the faster flow escaping below the reservoir in the Tongue River proper, there were rumored (always the rumors with fishing) to be more smallmouth bass, along with a very few rainbows and browns. All in all, a curious place to be.

Way over in this isolated, rarely visited corner of Montana, the only people you are likely to run across (or over—life's pace is slow in these parts) are members of the Northern Cheyenne living on the Reservation, ranchers, and devoted seekers of miles and miles of unchecked emptiness. Running right up and confronting the truth forced me to admit that this was my kind of place. So when a cassette on the finer points of turkey-calling arrived in the mail from Steve two days prior to the hunt, I packed the truck and struck out for Billings and a rendezvous with Steve.

Listening to the tape as I headed into Billings on I90 was interesting in an eye-opening sort of way. I heard, mixed in with an assortment of chirps, purts, and putts, that the birds can run thirty-five miles an hour, fly at over forty, hear and see ten times better than I ever dreamed, and have a 270-degree range of vision. Coupled with the facts that turkeys often weigh more than twenty pounds and fend off rivals and predators with large knife-edged spurs protruding from their ostrichlike legs, these were the makings of a formidable creature.

What had I gotten myself into? Wild turkeys and mad goldfish? Where was Trout Haven and the food pellets when sanity began slipping away?

Steve was in good form as we transferred my gear into the van. He'd just finished competing in the state's Peaks and Prairies Race, where teams ride bikes, paddle kayaks, and run sizeable distances in exhausting pursuit of a neat T-shirt and very little recognition. He'd placed in the top ten in the boating portion of the event and radiated a healthy glow to prove it. A pair of kayaks and a couple of mountain bikes were mounted on a rack above the van's roof. Well-equipped turkey hunters everywhere would appreciate this rig.

We headed away down the interstate under dark clouds and a touch of cold rain. The highway stretching east at Crow Agency was a good road with no sign of humans after a few miles. We passed an obelisk marking the site of the Battle of the Little Bighorn. Then the road broke away into mud and slop and we careered madly past huge earth-moving equipment. For the next hour we slipped and slided our way east, finally escaping the gumbo road-under-construction goofiness and returning to paved bliss. There were plenty of antelope and a vagrant raven or two, but that was it except for brief bursts of life in towns like Busby and Lame Deer, where a number of residents stopped dead in their tracks at the sight of us, stunned no doubt by the realization that world-class white water and top-notch mountain biking must be somewhere nearby.

Some more supplies were purchased in Ashland, and conversation over a beer and a shot in the local bar with a couple of the locals turned up a few choice locations for the goldfish (yes, the people down here knew of this fishing, too) and smallmouth bass. That gleam was back in Steve's eyes, which meant this trip was still in the crazy-conception phase rather than the full-blown out-of-control stage. Goldfish in spring were lurking on today's breezy horizon.

Steve navigated precisely to last year's campsite up on a bench in the middle of a grove of very old ponderosa. Rugged, fantastic eroded bluffs, ridges, and deep coulees sailed away with the clearing sky in all directions, playing an extremely subtle variation on a red, yellow, and brown color scheme. A well-worn volcanic cone was the beacon that guided Steve home.

You know you're in the middle of isolation proper when everything is so damn quiet there is a roaring in your ears until they adjust to the silence.

This really was nice country, and we'd spotted a small flock of turkeys feeding in a field. The birds raced along a barbed-wire fence and then up a ridge with unreal speed when they spotted us rounding a bend several hundred yards away. These guys would be tough to corner, especially on their home turf. I figured if the eight birds in the group averaged fifteen pounds each, we'd just observed over one hundred pounds of turkey. My imagination had a twisted field day with visions of a somber scene played at home with my wife and kids.

"Mom, what happened to Dad?" they would ask.

"Your father was killed when a herd of turkeys stampeded. He couldn't get out of the way fast enough and they ran over him."

Reality rarely plays a significant role in my outdoor experiences.

We pitched camp, reloaded our fishing gear, and headed for the reservoir down some bumpy, dusty roads, then along a few twisted miles of aging pavement before we turned onto a two-tracked bit of slop that led to the water.

We both rigged up 7-weights to counter the strong breeze, and Steve began working a large Muddler along and through the beginnings of this season's weed beds. He started taking pike immediately and was soon laughing and shouting with each five-to eight-pound fish that slashed and thrashed in the spring sunshine.

I, on the other hand, in pursuit of much craftier game tied on a #14 Gold-Ribbed Hare's Ear nymph and began stripping retrieves through a large hole in the weed growth that seemed to indicate a cold spring—a location, I'd been told by the boys in the bar, where the goldfish liked to hang out. The nymph failed to sink deep enough, so I switched to one of Jim Teeny's sinking tip lines, and that turned the trick. On the first cast a goldfish took, and for the next fifteen or twenty seconds I fought the powerful creature, who finally came to me floating on its side. I was exhausted, but not so tired that I failed to admire the creature's dirty whites, off-color oranges, and faded browns. A truly gorgeous fifteen-inch fish, and I hoped there would be many more.

But there weren't, and I think that is part of the magic and attraction of trophy goldfishing—you know the monsters are in there, but getting them to take is another matter entirely. I realize that one man's goldfish is another man's carp, but this really was interesting fishing, especially when compared to the mountain trout angling of my home turf. Variety is nice.

"Holt, you're sick."

"How so?"

"Anyone who drives six hundred miles to catch a goldfish is a troubled person."

"Perhaps, but God, can they fight."

"I noticed."

We returned to camp, but on our way stopped to fish some of the faster riffles and runs of the off-color river below the dam. We took a dozen bass of about one pound on weighted Muddlers worked quickly from casts made quartering upstream. The small-mouths were strong, as is their fashion, but somewhat dull in color, probably a result of adaptation to their cloudy environment. When you think about it, the past few hours had been pretty damn good fishing—northerns and smallmouths in abundance and a serious goldfish. I'd experienced a lot worse action in much uglier surroundings. No trout though, and it was difficult to imagine the fish hanging out in this dirty stuff, but who knows? We'd try again tomorrow after chasing a bird or two.

We were up at dawn and on our turkey-hunting way with only the soft crunching of the long pine needles making any sound. Dropping swiftly into a coulee defined by rock and earth of yellow and white, we moved down a dry stream-course that was a stairway of smooth, slabbed rock. Even in spring this area was dry, and I had a hard time believing that there were goldfish and pike and bass in the Tongue River Reservoir, less than an hour away.

The routine was simple. Walk for several minutes. Stop and make a croaking, scratching sound on the wooden box that was a turkey call. *Screech, screech, screech, screech* in rapid succession. Then wait for an answer, and when none came, repeat the pattern before moving on.

An hour of this and the morning was growing light, but it was just 7:30, so we walked on up to the point of a long open bluff that gave way to a view of more bluffs, ravines, and rolling parkland. In the distance, open-range cattle, black and brown ones, slowly munched away, bellowing periodically with the sound softened by the space between us.

Steve scratched his call, and far away a gobbler answered. The sound, one that I find laughable in a barnyard, was wild, exciting. There really were huge birds wandering around out here. The turkey called to us again. Elk bugling in the mountains of the Canadian Rockies in autumn is like this. The bird must have been miles away from us, strutting in the trees covering a slope climbing toward a buff-colored bench across the riftlike valley we were scanning.

Several minutes passed with no other noise from the turkey, despite some realistic screechings from Steve's call. We'd lost contact with the guy, who was probably chasing the proverbial bird in the hand instead of our long-distance offering. But that was not the end of this sequence, because a large gray-white object flashed through the pines below us, then vanished before reappearing less than thirty feet away.

A coyote as large as a wolf, with an immaculate fluffy coat pulled to a stop and stared at us with black eyes, at first confused at the anomaly. The animal had come to the sound of Steve's calling thinking turkey, but had discovered an obviously unfamiliar sight of humans. Motionless, he assessed the situation. We were frozen for what seemed like minutes, but the mood was timeless. Then he was gone. Just silently, totally gone.

"Wow. Did you see that? He thought we were turkeys," said Steve as his grin flashed bright in the cool light. "That was great. Let's go back and have some coffee."

For now the morning was enough and we saw feathers and droppings from the birds as we crossed a small stagnant pool of water before climbing up to our camp. The sky was clear, and colors that did not show yesterday lit up the country. All kinds of shades of green flickered through the wild grasses and in the pines. Blues shimmered above and the rocks and ridges glowed with orange, salmon, and ochre. Even lousy instant coffee tastes great under these conditions.

The middle of a blue-sky day is never prime time for anything wild, including trout, deer, and turkeys, so we piled into the van and headed back down the road for a little through-the-windshield exploration, which led us to a roadside home-maybe-general-store-possibly-post-office perched next to a red dirt road beside a small creek. A large dog was sleeping under a weathered wood bench. When Steve reappeared from within the store with a bag of corn curls and two cold beers, we went over and sat down.

The mail truck arrived, and the woman driving the thing stopped in front of us.

"Working hard I see. You must be over here hunting turkeys."

"It shows?"

"Well, nobody comes over here and sits on that bench drinking beer before noon if they're headed anywhere with some purpose in mind," she joked.

"God! Not even noon and we're not foolin' anybody. This is not good, John."

"Is there any more beer in the cooler in there?"

"Yes."

I'd heard that turkey hunting was a tough sport.

We headed back to the Tongue and once again the northerns cooperated, for both of us this time. I tried some likely looking goldfish holes with no success, and had it not been for the fish yesterday, I would have thought the rumors to be false or, at worst, intentionally misleading. Next year I'd chase these marginally legendary fish once more.

As for the pike, any streamer—Muddler, Bugger, Zonker—caught fish, and the biggest seemed just short of ten pounds. Like the smallmouths down below in the river, these fish were not brightly colored but rather a more subdued green that bordered on olive drab. But the pike were firm, healthy, full of fight, and present in good number. I'd definitely rather fish for rainbows on the Missouri. Still, this was fun, and it was finally spring outside and we were having a blast, so the hell with fly-fishing purism.

In the river the smallmouths cooperated again and we even took a couple on nymphs dead-drifted near the surface. The obvious conclusion was that the fish in this area were not used to streamers or nymphs and that as long as the water did not warm up and/or turn to liquid dirt, the fishing would be steady if not actually very good.

A breezy, take-it-easy kind of afternoon suggested a siesta until the evening's efforts. Therm-a-Rest fantasies shimmered in the seductive atmosphere.

The decision was made to drive down the dirt lane a mile or so from camp, split up, and go in opposite directions to cover more ground and, I think, to give Steve the chance to work alone. The clickings and whirrings of my camera were making him a bit edgy.

Working down another rocky draw, I turned up the feathered remains of a turkey that did not escape the hungry attentions of the area's coyote population. I wondered if all of the birds had been eaten around here while I labored up a timbered ridge and onto still another bench that gave way to still another wide valley. The evening was warm and dead-still and the heightened hues of sunset were cloaking the countryside. I could hear cattle but nothing else.

Then, over a ridge to the west, the sound of turkeys. I called back and a few minutes later received an answer, this time much nearer. Could my novice attempts at sounding like a female turkey actually be fooling this male?

The birds would bolt at the slightest movement, so I hunkered down with my back against a big old pine and made another call. The bird answered only a few hundred yards below. I waited, scarcely breathing, for another response. Too much calling, the voice on the cassette had warned, would send turkeys running for cover. Minutes later a somewhat familiar bird sounded in a copse of pines below a small knoll. Was this man or turkey, I wondered?

Camouflaged hunters blasted each other to oblivion all of the time Back East, but Steve should be a few miles west of me.

Screech screech screech screech.

I waited, silently. The noise sure sounded natural enough, but there was a slight feeling that something was wrong here (swift realizations on the high plains).

Screech screech screech screech.

I was pretty sure that this was not a wild bird, and an insight that turkey-hunting might possibly be a metaphor for some larger aspects of living was gathering painful momentum.

Screech screech screech screech.

"Steve?"

"Oh damn. I wondered if that was you."

Turkey hunters hunting each other and calling in coyotes all in the space of twelve hours. This was strange sport we were engaged in out here.

The sky was darkening and the temperature dropping as we walked back to the van. Jackrabbits bounded in and out of our headlights on the way back to camp. Things were not looking good as far as a successful hunt was concerned, and Steve concluded that we had "to do more things right," which translated into rising around two hours before dawn in order to hit likely looking turkey turf before first light.

We backed up to our tents, turned off the engine, and I jumped out of the van in search of my cigars and a beer. Something was weird. Focused so hard and long on listening for gobbling, the sounds coming from the pines just behind camp did not register right off.

Gobble, gobble, gobble in gay profusion. There must be over a hundred turkeys heading for roost trees within the length of a football field from us. They'd been here all the time. We'd found turkey-hunter paradise.

"Steve. Get out of the damn truck. There are turkeys all over the place."

We listened. This was a raucous riot of turkey talk — gobblings, putts, and purts sailed through the near darkness. Never have I heard such a wild, untamed, chaotic symphony.

We could not help but laugh for a long time until I eventually found a pair of beers and got my cigar torched to a fiery, smoking blaze.

By now everything was silence. The turkeys were in bed in their ponderosa lodges. Everything was washed in an instrument-panel-green glow. The trees, the van, our tents cast deep shadows.

Overhead, in the direction of Billings, the sky blazed in sheet after sheet and countless waves of northern lights. The display was of such intensity that I could read "Cuban made" on my cigar's band. And the lights did not let up for over an hour, then they suddenly quit, rushing up and away from us over the North Pole, leaving the blazing band of the Milky Way behind.

Just your average night in Montana somewhere. We crawled into our tents eager for tomorrow.

Steve was up and off in the dark. I stayed behind to make coffee and prepare my camera gear to shoot the dead turkey that I was sure my friend would return with. It was cold and you could smell rain in the air.

Thirty minutes passed. Then another fifteen as the sky showed dawn and the sound of rising turkeys rose from over the hill.

Kaboom. And then again, *Kaboom.* The unmistakable sound of heavy-duty twelve-gauge turkey loads. Then dead silence for long minutes before I spotted Steve with a large bird draped over his shoulders. He was shaking with the excitement of the hunt and the shooting.

"They were all over the place. Everywhere. There must have been eighty or a hundred just beyond that ridge strutting in a park-like area. I mean, I could have shot dozens of turkeys out there. They were everywhere."

The rain was with us now and very cold as Steve field-dressed the bird and we broke camp amid cries of retreat. The weather had turned ugly with a vengeance, and we did not have time to enjoy anything. Packing up everything was wet, numbing business, and the sound of the heater going full-tilt in the van was the carrot that kept us moving. No more fishing or hunting on this trip. A spring storm was on us hard-core, right now.

As soon as we hit the dirt "road," we knew we were in big trouble. The van wanted to lurch and slide into the nearest ditch. The rain-now-raging-snowstorm had turned the top inch or so of dirt into treacherous, slippery paste. We made one slight rise and were almost dead in the water when I hopped out and pushed, gaining another quarter-mile before the van began to spin its wheels.

I was soaked and covered with mud and Steve was soon in the same shape as we sloshed around putting on chains, which moved us a little nearer the top of the hill before the whole mess slogged to a halt on the edge of the road.

We scanned the map with survivalist intensity as the windows fogged up and our clothes turned delightfully clammy.

"We're going to have to walk for it, Steve."

"I know. It's not going to get any better. We could be here for days."

Some clown on the radio confirmed this assessment with a cutesy, humorous reading of a weather forecast that called for lots and lots of snow and wind during the next few days in southeastern Montana.

We finished the lukewarm coffee in our thermos and forced down a couple of chewy bagels before striking out in the blizzard. At the top of the hill we turned to look back at the van, both wondering if we'd see it again. We could barely make out the shape of the thing now with all of the snow flying around.

"What do you think? Are we making a mistake?"

The van was covered in snow by now.

"Let's give it one more try. Are you up to pushing?"

"You just get that sucker moving. I'll push 'til hell freezes over," which was apparently not that far away.

Steve gunned the engine. I shoved. The chains dug through the mud. The van started to move. The rubbery smell of well-done clutch filled the air. The van moved faster and I was now running to keep up as we neared the top of the rise.

The passenger door swung open and I heard "Jump in. I can't stop," and I did, banging my kneecap and forehead on assorted metal parts in the process.

This was big time now. We'd either hit the "main" gravel road a few miles ahead or roll in a ditch trying. Neither of us wanted to face an extended walk in this stuff.

The van slid and swerved back and forth like a crazed Beaver-head River brown trout as Steve madly swung the wheel while goosing the accelerator and touching the brakes at appropriate junctures in the pretty-much-out-of-control tour through the sage-brush prairie.

In what seemed like two years, but took less than fifteen minutes, we cruised through the slush to a stop sign that heralded (and there should have been blaring trumpets and well-dressed public officials for this one) a return to a halfway-decent road.

"Ashland's in the bag," was the cry. The chains made travel through the half-foot of wet snow relatively easy. A sign, dripping the wet stuff, declared "Ashland — 8 miles."

Rounding a swinging curve in the wide road now running through thick forest, that small town and its dark bar looked very nice in my mind's eye. I'd love to talk goldfish with the boys in there. But hold on a second . . .

"Whoa there, John. Look at all those turkeys standing in the road," and the grin was back in full force, its glare blowing away my Ashland dreamscape.

Unzipping my gun case, I grabbed the beat-up Savage .20, dropped down out of the van, and started running through the snow after the flock of turkeys that were fast disappearing, some-where in the frenzy of blinding snowflakes, just out of range . . .

Sweet Grass Hills

*T*he world according to trout as I remember it is gone. Sedate evenings shooting tight loops over placid lakes to discreetly rising cutthroats are things of a murky past.

There is chaos here reigning unchecked beneath the eerie glow of the Milky Way. Blackfeet Indian ghosts dance lunatic rhythms on the low ridge connecting Middle and East Buttes, too far out here to be anything but real in the Sweet Grass Hills. Diaphanous spirits shimmer in a northern lights glow. Magic land for this tribe. The wind is roaring its low level version of clear air turbulence for a confused, wide-eyed fly fisher.

The reassuring amenities of a Conoco station in distant Sunburst are lying out of reach many miles to the west. How I miss those pop, candy, and cigarette machines lined up along its front wall. Colorful images of Coke, Orange Crush, Mars Bars (perhaps some foreshadowing here), Camel straights, Chesterfields. And those impressive displays of new radial tires and mounds of oil cans in a staggering array of viscosities, familiar delights radiating the transient security of an earlier life, now beyond my grasp.

The surface of this small reservoir is alive with feeding fish. Rainbows gone berserk. Mad with the wind and the iced charge of starlight. I can hear them chewing up the water. Each cast takes a trout—twelve inches, sixteen inches, twenty inches. One fish leaps from the pond and hits my damsel nymph in midair. I can see this clearly in the soft blue-white light. My shadow mocks me as it vibrates in the grass.

Never have I had a night of fishing like this. Not casting large
plugs to mean muskies on a dark northern Wisconsin August night.
Not tubing for bass under a full moon. This is distant country.
I have never been here before.

There is fear of something unknown mixed in with the excitement, and I love it. All anglers deserve at least one out-of-control
night like this each season. Nothing is predictable, as is proper,
and the fishing is fine.

Getting to this place and these hills is not easy. The trip spanned
years of distant curiosity, a little map work, and plenty of stops
to ask for directions. The Sweet Grass Hills have always piqued
my imagination. They sit right up next to the Alberta border looking like long-dormant volcanoes. Every time I raced east or west
along the Hi-Line through towns like Cut Bank, Shelby, Lothair,
and Inverness, I wondered if there were trout swimming away
somewhere in those hills. Maybe in small creeks or perhaps in
out-of-the-way lakes or maybe in a farm pond or two.

The hills dominate the skyline. Millions of acres of wheat fields
roll away across the plains in every direction. Few people live out
here, and even Interstate 15 heading dead-straight north and south
makes little impact on the vastness and refined loneliness. Turn
off the paved roads. Drive down a dusty path. Stop. Get out and
listen. The silence, except for a puff of air rustling the wheat, is
strong stuff. After mere minutes the sound of a meadowlark talking
in the brushy ditch over there by the county-road sign sounds like
the finest jazz.

What spaced-out, powerful land. I sure as hell would not want
to live here. January must be interesting. But what calm and
majesty on a warm summer day.

The Sweet Grass Hills consist of three main buttes—West,
Middle, and East. The tallest, West Butte at 6,983 feet, is more
than 300 feet higher than Logan Pass on Going-to-the-Sun Road
in Glacier National Park. East Butte at 6,958 feet is a dead ringer
for a volcanic cone. Each is a downsized mountain range made
up of igneous rock that flowed out of the earth's crust. This rock
formed about 50 million years ago; feldspar, sodium, and potassium

are present in quantity. Sedimentary rocks surround it. During the Bull Lake ice age, more than seventy thousand years ago, the continental glacier flowed around the three buttes. Now they stand like islands adrift in an earthen sea.

Powerful forces formed the hills. The energy is obvious as soon as I get out of the car halfway up a dirt lane that winds around Grassy Butte. A peaceful place. Images of the land without homes and lights fill my head. Waves of blue-green grass bend in the evening breeze. No clouds. The setting sun casts a copper glow on dozens of ranch ponds scattered among the gentle depressions in the terrain below.

My friend hikes off into the grass. I see his figure grow smaller and smaller as he climbs higher. Eventually he disappears over a distant ridge now bathed in orange light. The wind blows cool as it drifts down the hills. I light a Jamaican cigar and watch the smoke glide away from me on the invisible stream. The reservoir we are seeking is still hidden from us. We stopped at four ranch homes and asked for directions. The youngest person we spoke with was over seventy, the oldest past ninety. They all smiled and knew where we were going (we did not). They all asked if we liked mosquitoes, and two of them added that they had not been to the part of the hills we were seeking for many years. Each stop turned up a few more twists and turns pointed out with arm gesticulations and smiles that brought us closer to our goal, a small piece of water that rumor claimed was filled with big rainbows. Actually, tales of a number of ponds in the region offered similar glories. This one was picked at random. We had to begin somewhere.

We were now miles back into the hills and hundreds of feet above a valley filled with grain and hay fields. Hungarian partridge hens with their large broods of fist-sized chicks wandered all over the place. Deer floated through the grass. A large frog croaked in a bog below some old mine tailings.

As I finished setting up camp, I knew we would find the lake tomorrow. I finished my cigar while watching lightning flashing silently from distant purple clouds that swirled far beyond West Butte across the border in Canada.

A small Sweet Grass Hills reservoir with East Butte in the background.

The next morning we broke camp and followed what remained of a dirt track down and around East Butte, through a narrow place called Mosquito Draw. Weathered fence lay collapsed on both sides of us, exhausted from years of fighting the climate. Pockets of water covered in a greenish scum drew flies in the low spots of the ravine. Only nine in the morning and already warm. Maybe one hundred degrees by afternoon. A large swampy pond appeared on our right. No trout here, I was sure.

Then, bending left, we came around a grass- and sage-covered hill. The reservoir stretched for about twenty-five acres from its earthen impoundment on one end to its tapered, narrow terminus in a meadow at the other. A tiny creek trickled in here right next to a crumbling log structure. Dense aquatic plant growth reached the water's surface in a ten-foot-wide band about twenty feet from shore. Holes in this stuff seemed to indicate springs. Small trout fed on very small insects. Damselflies and a few caddis were in the air. East Butte towered above us. The only signs of humans were the fence lines and the "road" we came in on. We set up camp. I rigged my 5-weight while my friend began reading a book. Fly fishing is not an important part of his life, but he likes to camp and has a marginally funny sense of humor—a worthwhile companion on a trip such as this one.

Casting to the feeding fish in a small bay with a #22 Comparadun, I took a number of eight- to ten-inch rainbows. Fun at first, but not what I was here for. The temperature cruised past ninety and even this action slowed. There must be larger trout here. There was good water, though a bit green with algae bloom. There were plenty of insects. Switching to a #10 damsel nymph, I cast along the edge of the weed growth parallel to the shore and allowed the weighted pattern to sink down several feet. Even with the algae I could see the fly. Retrieving the slack, I jerked the nymph slightly a couple of times. Mouth wide open, body shining silver, a large rainbow streaked from cover and hit the damsel. The trout broke the surface with the set and jumped and thrashed at my feet before being netted. Eighteen inches, firm but a bit on the large-headed side of life, an indication that the reservoir might be overcrowded and the population running in the stunted direction. So what? There were fish of size here and I needed a bigger one badly. I went back toward the car and our tents in search of my box of larger damsel nymphs. I found cold beer immediately and a #8 nymph a little later. I stayed with 5X tippet and a leader of around ten feet—my own knotted construction that was soft and pliable, allowing the damsel to swim like a snake in the water, the way it should.

For the next few hours, well into the midday heat, I worked the channel between shore and the plants, taking dozens of trout from twelve to over twenty inches. Hell, I know this is not the thrilling match-the-hatch action of the Letort or the chase-of-the-big-browns game on the Missouri in October, but catching these rainbows while cooking under a hot sun with no one watching except for the slightly solemn presence of East Butte was pleasurable fun, and I knew that one more location was now on my yearly angling itinerary.

Taking a break around two, I wandered across the sage toward the swampy pond. Ducks streaked from my approach and popped into the air, making a racket. A badger poked its head from a large hole in a low mound, then scuttled back into the darkness. Buttercups and other flowers blossomed all over the place. The smell of sage filled the dry air. Flies buzzed and bees hummed among the ground cover. A large blue-gray heron broke its standstill routine and lifted skyward, leading my gaze to a pair of vultures working the thermals far above, the dihedral angle of their wings clearly visible despite the great altitude. Returning to camp I saw my friend practicing Tai Chi on a bluff overlooking the water—a most curious sight out here, but then we are all eccentric to some extent.

The setting sun threw an orange-bronze blood red radiance over the hills. A family of Canada geese cautiously worked their way along the far shore, then through the grass and out of sight. Evening sailed into night. My friend went to sleep. I smoked a cigar and watched the silhouettes of a herd of antelope grazing a ridge below the butte. The stars came out and I marveled at the thought that there were hundreds (thousands?) of little lakes like this scattered about Montana east of the Continental Divide waiting to be discovered and fished. A most pleasant realization. I looked at my watch. Almost midnight. The wind had kicked up in the last hour, ruffling the water down below, and small waves flashed in the low light. The sudden awareness of unrestrained splashing and the sight of riseforms all over the reservoir made me jump up for a closer look. With a subtlety that belied the feeding frenzy now taking place, the lake had come alive with crazed rainbows. I could see large ones leaping and then crashing back into the water. I staggered over to the tent and grabbed the rod, then tripped and stumbled my way to the water.

And that's where I came in at the beginning. Casting and catching trout steadily. Some of the fish over twenty inches. This was indeed crazy in a lovely, angling sort of way. The riot lasted for maybe an hour and then just stopped. In an instant. Some natural (or maybe unnatural) motion had clicked into place and

*Jon Heberling thanks the angling gods for this rainbow taken
in the Sweet Grass Hills.*

halted the feeding. The wind still blew, but the rainbows were gone. East Butte was a dark force on the horizon. The antelope were gone. A thick black bank of clouds was moving in from the north. Enough for tonight. In my tent I savored the weird fishing. The storm hit with winds gusting to the point that they compressed the walls of my tent together. I felt like Patrick McGoohan, in the British TV series "The Prisoner," when he was captured by that large white balloonlike "guardian."

Morning came and the rough weather was off southeast somewhere. A beautiful day as they say. The reservoir was calm except for a few rising trout and the Canada geese paddling along shore. We packed and headed back toward the Rocky Mountain Front and home. I began to wonder if last night had really happened. The distance of a few hours made all of the wildness seem far away.

The Sweet Grass Hills. My Indian friends were right. They do resonate special magic.

Merrell Lake

*T*he story goes that you have to be brain dead not to catch a rainbow of several pounds or more at private Merrell Lake, located behind Hubbard's Yellowstone Lodge.

The tale is true. The fishing I've experienced here is filled with fat rainbows that hit nymphs, drys, Buggers, and just about anything else winged out into the middle of the spring-fed eighty-acre lake. Patterns tossed toward shore do all right, too. Rainbows to eight pounds are taken here. I've seen a number in the three-to-five range.

Sure, I know, this is a private place and it costs good money to spend time here.

So what?

Guides on a river cost money. Fly rods cost money. Bail bondsmen cost money. Tickets to watch the Cubs play at Wrigley are a waste of money.

The whole setup sits on a ridge that gives way to completely adequate views of the surrounding mountains and the Paradise Valley drifting away far below.

The lovely Paradise Valley. How do you describe this piece of off-the-wall-ville to someone who has never been here?

Well, The Church Universal and Triumphant (CUT) makes its home here. These are the people who built bomb shelters all over the place because the world was going to end in October of 1989. Perhaps it did, so maybe they are right. And this crew also polluted a fine cutthroat spawning stream with improperly installed

23

Fishing Merrell Lake in April.

underground fuel tanks. A lot of these individuals are on the run from the law and one or two are purported to carry guns. Almost all of them dress mostly in purple. A finer group of people does not walk the planet.

And there's more.

Like the boys who illegally gather shed elk horn lying on the ground (mostly, they shoot the animals and cut the horn afterward) in Yellowstone Park just down the road from the Lodge. The horn is used to make real neat cribbage boards and stuff. This bunch has been known to bloody each other over prime turf. Gathering elk horn is fun.

And the drug runners in the little old long-dead mining town of Jardine just up the mountain east of Gardiner are fun on occasion—whackos so far gone that they once freaked out a former state cop turned private detective. He was asking questions about a missing person last seen up there, but the pervasive weirdness and malevolence were so strong he shakily pulled out his

.38 Special, backed into his car, and beat cheeks back down the hill in a cloud of brown dust.

Gorgeous country.

Sane people.

The good life.

As usual, I digress. Back to the fishing, which is prime in the valley's spring creeks, in the Yellowstone River, in the park, and, of course, up on the Lodge's holdings. Spend a month here and you'll stumble into a nice angling rhythm of fish, eat, fish, have a beer, fish, have a few cocktails and a big dinner, have another drink and go to bed to sleep forever or at least eight hours. Still, you would only have had a taste of the Merrell Lake rainbows, the surprising browns that hit a Gray Wulff like lunatics (and I can seriously appreciate this) in nearby Tom Miner Creek, of tagging a few rainbows (browns in the autumn) on the Gardner above town, and a hell of a lot more.

The first time I saw Merrell Lake came about as the result of a speaking engagement I had up the valley at Pray. This was the first and, I swear on my brother's grave (wherever it is), the last time I will ever get up in front of a room full of people and try to deliver a coherent speech. This type of recreation is for those built of sterner stuff than I.

Anyway, there are a number of things I never expected to find in this state. Such as a good restaurant at the old resort sitting beside a dead-end highway beneath Emigrant Peak in the southwestern quadrant of the state a few minutes north of Yellowstone National Park. Montana is home to often seriously overcooked cheeseburgers and way underdone lamb chops, so when I walked into the Chico Hot Springs Lodge at Pray late one night several years ago, I was taken aback to discover a menu offering mushrooms stuffed with escargot, artichokes with horseradish sauce, and Cajun shrimp before Cajun was passé.

As I pulled up to the parking area, the sight of dozens of men and women casting fly rods on the front lawn seemed anomalous even for this part of the world. Bright yellow fly lines filled the chilly air. The style of clothing favored by these landlocked fly casters leaned toward plaid shirts, blue jeans, and cowboy hats. There were also a number of people wearing waxed-cotton coats as protection against the brisk April wind and swirling snowflakes. A white-muzzled yellow Lab watched the action while lying under the front porch overhang.

This was a gathering of guides and outfitters from around the country, here to attend discussions and seminars on how to run a better fly-fishing service operation that would insure repeat business from their clients (paying fly fishers). Just then, those outside were trying out the sponsoring company's newest fly rods. I was to be part of the panel presentation titled "Guides' and Outfitters' Role in Promoting Fish and Game Conservation."

Following a fine meal, I retreated to the lounge and examined the gathering's schedule. Seminar topics included "Controlling Expectations," "Guiding Opportunities in Saltwater Fishing," and "The Power of a Guide's Suggestion in Tackle Shop Sales." Several guides were sitting at a nearby table and they were particularly taken with a comment made during the "Female Clients—A Guide's Delight" presentation by the woman speaker, who said that wearing neoprene waders on the river during the heat of a summer day was uncomfortable and suggested that perhaps the sponsoring company should be "on the cutting edge" and design a line of bikini fly-fishing wear. I finished my drink and went up to my room.

The next morning at the panel discussion three intent-looking individuals (I was the sweaty one slumping stage right) were seated at a table on a raised platform. The one in the middle, Robert Jones, is a regular contributor to *Sports Illustrated* and the author of several novels, including *Blood Sport*. Jones began the session by intoning, "Be prepared for an hour of doom and gloom." He was not kidding.

Bob pretty much summed up the world as it relates to fishing, big game, upland birds, and the environment. The picture was not a rosy one, as anyone who read his special report for Audubon called "Farewell to Africa" in 1990 will appreciate. He lays out the facts and lets the chips fall where they will and the hell with yupsters, New-Agers, and other confused flotsam. He's not an apologist for our race. He just doesn't have time for bullshit when something he cares about, like trout, is being destroyed by greed, ignorance, and overpopulation. I like Bob and we've become friends in a long-distance-Ma-Bell, maybe-fish-together-once-a-year sort of way.

His was a tough act to follow. I did not do all that well, but then I did not make a break for the back door, either. Not one for public speaking, I was nervous as hell, despite a couple of pre-game-warm-up Bloody Marys. The only words that I remember speaking were my first ones.

"We have a certifiable lunatic for a governor in Montana."

To this day that particular governor does not like me much. (In fact, he only served one term in office.) He can take a number with the rest of them.

Silvio Calabi, editor and publisher of *Fly Rod & Reel,* finished on a slightly more upbeat note. Then the three of us retired to the bar for a few more before heading to Merrell for some casual angling.

The Tom Miner Basin road climbing to Merrell Lake heads off west just above Yankee Jim Canyon. The way leads up swiftly on several switchbacks, each one revealing a fresh perspective on owner Jim Hubbard's thirteen-thousand-acre spread. The main lodge is a large, modern, log structure with a flying bridge running the length of the main room, which serves as lounge, bar, living room.

Merrell Lake used to freeze out every couple of years or so whenever an especially harsh Montana winter blasted through the area. The trout were then wiped out from oxygen starvation. Hubbard cured the problem by aerating the lake, and the process creates immense waves of bubbles percolating about various locations on the lake. The first sight of this process made me wonder if some sort of Loch Nessian monster were about to breach the surface. No problems with *my* grip on reality.

Merrell is fecund, with abundant weed growth at one end. Trout cruise this shallow south shore in search of midges and damsels.

Silvio Calabi casts to Merrell Lake rainbows.

A Sheep Creek pitched toward shore and slowly retrieved with
slight undulations works okay (as it does in any lake of this type).
Caddis pupae imitations also produce. The Chironomids provide
nice evening hatch action in #14 to #16. If the fly you are using
matches the size of the hatch but the trout ignore it, move up one
size larger. This is true on lakes for midges, caddis, and to a lesser
extent, mayflies. On streams the tendency is to drop down a size.

Because this is a closed system that is carefully managed, fishing
sculpin or other forage fish patterns does not come into play as
it would on many other lakes, where working inlets and outlets
often turns the biggest fish of the lake.

Distance is not really required here. Neither are shooting heads,
which really help reach distant cruising trout on larger waters.

Woolly Buggers also produce. So well, in fact, that *Fly Fisherman* editor and publisher John Randolph says fishing the pattern
"is like throwing a wine bottle in a drunk tank."

There are also *Callibaetis* here, and they begin around August.

Gold-Ribbed Hare's Ears in #16 to #18 handle the nymph action. Light Cahills, Adamses, and Comparaduns cover the dry action.

We pulled in, greeted our hosts, unloaded and rigged rods, then headed for the lake. Bob went off in one boat. Silvio and I struck out in another—a small aluminum job with electric motor. We cruised west past the lodge and Silvio immediately began casting some sort of sparkle nymph toward shore while I took photos. Within a minute or so he hooked a nice plump fish that thrashed the surface of the dark green water.

"These fish . . . you could probably tie on a big Gray Ghost and catch them. This is not bad," commented Silvio as he shot a cast toward a brushy bank while taking in the view. A rainbow boiled and took on the first strip. Plenty of below-the-surface flashings and tuggings, then a curved leap and some broken-water behavior. Three pounds, maybe a bit more. The trout was released and we both smiled. Smooth sailing here.

This was repeated throughout the afternoon as the sun shafted through the clouds and snow squalls highlighted the peaks with constantly shifting perspectives toned light and dark, blue and green, gold and silver. The fishing was steady for spirited chunky rainbows and the weather, though brisk, was not unpleasant.

After a while everyone returned to shore and the lodge for some refreshment, a little BS, and some of the best views of the Rocky Mountains found this side of paradise.

I could think of plenty worse ways to kill off a month.

Lake X

*F*our straight days of wind and cold. Very few fish. Early April along the Rocky Mountain Front is proving difficult this year. The four of us have been throwing streamers, nymphs, and, in desperation, even drys to large rainbows that make brief appearances next to shore in shallow water.

Ice-out on the Blackfeet Reservation and the fishing has not gone south. Apparently it never came north. Daylight to dark and we've taken four trout among us, the biggest approaching four pounds.

When the breeze calms to twenty-five miles per hour you can almost cast. These moments of halcyon conditions are brief, fleeting. Blasts of icy air come whistling down from the snow-covered mountains and freight-train their way across the prairie. The wind almost knocks you off your feet at its strongest. Rocking back and forth in the gale is part of the routine.

Early spring is a time of the year when the big rainbows of this region move into the shallows to participate in their annual false-spawning ritual. There are few, if any, inlets and outlets in the lakes, reservoirs, and ponds out here, so the fish are responding from instinct and they are not replenishing their numbers.

Where are we? a sane person might ask.

Questions of geographical location are not especially relevant. It does not really matter. Every piece of water on the Reservation with any size and depth offers the same bizarre action. Call this place Lake X, but you could also call the water Mission or Duck. Big water that attracts the most attention from fly fishers because

30

of trout numbers and accessibility. Depending upon elevation, the severity of the just-completed winter, and the current weather, the water begins to free itself of ice beginning in March and ice-out fishing lasts sometimes into May. The trick is to be on the water shortly after the breakup. That is when the trout move close to shore. Too soon, like right now, and the fish will not take. Too late, and they have already moved back down into deeper water or are clustered around midlake upwellings of spring water.

You can see them come in. Dark submarine shapes cruising up from the depths and riding the white-capped waves. One minute the water is empty, the next a dozen or more trout are working toward you. They ride the swells into the wave-scoured gravel, now free of silt and detritus. From a high bank overlooking prime water a friend and I watch them form circles, daisy chains, and they flash aggressively back and forth along a hundred-foot bar of clean rock. Fish of a pound or so to much larger roam this area, sometimes slashing through a wave to sparkle briefly in the light before diving into the next wash of surf. The biggest males dominate the action, driving away the smaller ones. They butt and charge one another, sort of like a bar scene near closing time.

We split up and work our way cautiously into the water, perhaps fifty yards apart. We cast toward each other, and our streamers hit the water unnoticed by the rainbows. There is too much surface disturbance and the fish have other things on their minds.

Strip. Strip. Pause. Strip. Strip.

"Was that a take?" I shout above the weather. "I saw your rod tip jerk down."

"Yes, but they're hitting short."

That's been our fate. The sharp taps of rainbows hitting the ends of our Buggers, Zonkers, and Marabou Muddlers is maddening. I try stripping and then hesitating, hoping to time an unseen approach of an attacking fish, but the maneuver is unsuccessful. Slower retrieves. Faster strips. Nothing produces, and the failure is frustrating. I feel that I should take at least a few trout, if only as a reward for braving the nasty conditions, but there is no such

*Trying to fish Lake X on the Blackfeet Reservation during
an April hurricane: John Talia dons fins.*

justice and that is an honest part of fly fishing. Maintaining the
facade of "tough guy" does not earn bonus points.

The wind is a real problem for us and perhaps for the fish. A
float tube spins around on a lake like a cork. Water Otters — one-
man pontoon fishing platforms — cannot handle the turbulence.
In calm weather they are a joy to fish from, offering an excellent
view of the action and a sturdy, above-water casting position. This
wind threatens to capsize them. Working from shore is the only
realistic and safe approach to the angling at this point. There are
times, particularly beneath the higher banks, when we are sheltered
from the constant storm and can make fairly lengthy, accurate
casts. But these periods are limited.

It is obvious that we are on the fish, but maybe a week (or less)
too early. They have just moved into the shallows and are not
looking up or at anything but one another. At least that is what
we surmise over drinks at the end of the day in our motel rooms.

I took one fish on a Zonker. The rainbow was riding a wave near its crest, perhaps for the oxygen. My cast was initially off the mark, but a gust blew the thing right in front of the trout. What could it do but strike? The fish raced to deep water and I held on, wading carefully back to the safe footing of the sandy point over my shoulder. I pulled the trout to me. Solid, broad, and full of spawning color, the bright crimson of its gill plates were striking. The best fish of the trip for me. I caught one other while casting the gravel bar with my companion.

The success of the one fish renewed my enthusiasm and I kept casting into those rolling waves, now without trout. My friends worked up and down the shore and into a large inlet of cloudy blue water. Pelicans were lined on the inlet stream's banks looking for easy pickings, but none of us, including the birds, turned a rainbow — or a brown, for that matter.

After wearing down our casting arms, my friend and I climbed back up the bank and watched the whirling trout, an amazing spectacle. This was grizzly country, and the bears were probably out of their dens by now. A tangle of alder over a rise to our right looked promising and bear vibes were in the air, but that was all. Just vibes. Thankfully, no bears. I could not possibly outrun one of the creatures. They are as fast as quarter horses. The thought of lurching and clomping across the countryside in chest waders with a griz in hot pursuit was humorous in a dark sort of way. I've seen a few wandering the hills back up near the mountains at this lake. That is close enough for me. Bear encounters are not required entertainment on my fishing adventures.

"I just don't know, John. The fish are here. They just won't take. Interesting fishing. When I get home, I'm going to read up on this. There's a solution here, somewhere."

Other anglers that we spoke with in nearby Browning were also having a tough time. They shook heads, shrugged shoulders. Tight smiles that all serious anglers know well crossed their wind-burned faces.

Ice-out is a strange experience. Fish one week and participate in the ultimate in angling frustration — large fish working at your feet that will not spook, nor will they strike. Come back to the same water three days later and everything you throw turns a rainbow. Two days more and the fishing shuts down, and two days after that the action flares red-hot. Fishing the Reservation is always a crapshoot, but never more so than during the spring. This is a time to touch a really big trout, but the action is normally, even predictably, sparse.

I am glad I brought my 8-weight, and next year I will bring along some shooting heads to help me try and cheat the wind a little bit. Weighted streamers are sufficient for reaching the trout in the shallow water. Sink-Tips would be too much, leading to snags and break-offs on the rough bottom. Even in the gloom sunglasses are worn. The wind makes losing an eye a definite threat without protection. I have already nailed the back of my head once, and this felt quite good in a perverted sort of way. Feeling anything besides numbness in the cold was heartening. But what the hell — a new year's fishing has started and I am not cooped up in the house fondling fly rods or thumbing through ragged magazines about fly fishing. The warmer temperatures will be here soon enough. Days of a hundred degrees or more out here on the plains cooking my brains into deep-fried pork rinds. Sweet thoughts running riot in April.

During summer and early fall hatches of caddis, *Callibaetis*, damsels, and of course hoppers provide steady if not fine action. And leeches and Buggers and Hare's Ears also produce. Spring is different though. Big-trout hunting with no guarantee of success. Just ask my friends. Four days and four fish. That's all, and I feel a bit guilty for asking them up here. The weather is abysmal, tough, awful, miserable. Take your pick. These guys live to fish (and hunt), and they know how the game goes. No complaints. A little jive. Some laughter and good conversation. And plenty of hard fishing. They've learned to take the rough with the easy and I'm happy to have friends such as these. They are what fly fishing for me is all about. And so is the wildness of the Rocky Mountain Front towering above us in the west. Nothing much has changed out here. A few more roads and homes, but that's about the extent of man's intrusion for now. A threatened oil well in the nearby wilderness was shot down and the tribe is taking an active role in preserving the unspoiled nature of the land.

Earlier we tried fishing Mission Lake with no success. Others we watched went fishless also. We drove north to Duck Lake, but it was still frozen tight. Deep snowbanks covered the aspen trunks halfway up. We headed back toward town in a blizzard. Not a cheery type of day. On a trip here last year at about the same time the temperature neared eighty and I fished in waders with my shirtsleeves rolled up. Instead of being rubbed raw by the wind, I took in my first sunburn of the season. The fishing was slow then, too, but better than this, and a number of rainbows from two to five pounds were caught (and released). The countryside back then seemed like another world. Instead of dull brown and gray and dirty snow, the sky was deep blue. Fresh green sprouts were breaking through the hard ground. Puffy white clouds floated by overhead. I'll fish the Reservation anytime, but I prefer casting in sunshine and warmth and without tornadic gusts tearing my fly line in all directions at once. Serpentine casts of an unplanned nature grow old fast.

The following week I headed back over the Continental Divide, stopping at Marias Pass to take some photographs of the surrounding peaks and rapidly melting snow. The dirt road to Dupuyer was muddy in spots from the runoff, and the drive back to the lake took over an hour. No one was there. I put on my chest waders, rigged a 6-weight, and tied on a #2 Yellow Zonker. There was just a light breeze and the temperature was near seventy— summer compared to last week's winter. I walked around the lake to the gravel bar on the western shore and crept to the edge of the overlook. The fish were there. Maybe twenty, and a couple looked big; several pounds at least.

Wading into casting position well above the circling trout, I worked out enough line to cover them and shot a cast to the deep-water side of the rainbows, letting the streamer sink for a count of three (an arbitrary figure on my part). Two strips and a solid take. My rod tip vibrated back and forth and line spun off the reel

A nice Reservation rainbow.

as the drag made a great, screeching buzz. Music of the finest kind. One cast and a fish on. How things change out here. The trout leaped once. Twice. Then a series of quick jumps and flips. Silver-and-red and spots dancing in the sunlight. Some line in, then more torn off the reel. A good fish. Over twenty inches. Another quick blast of acrobatics and one more run. This was perfect. I heard myself yelling and laughing. A madman at peace with the world, if only briefly. The rainbow circled in on me, tired, drifting on its side. I measured the fish against the rod, marking the distance in my mind, then watched as the trout swam slowly but steadily out of sight into the deeper dark green water. I pulled out a sewing tape I'd taken from Lynda. Twenty-one inches. Not bad.

I cast again to the same spot, letting the Zonker sink, briefly. Stripped and another trout was on, leaping and crashing back to the surface, sending up crystalline rings of spray.

The sun kept on shining and the fish kept on hitting the Zonker. This was heaven and I knew I was home, again. If only my friends were here. They'd never believe this when I told them over the phone.

Flathead
Lake

*T*he thought of nymphing for whitefish in a huge deep lake is not high in the priorities of any sane angler, nor is it a driving force in my life.

Regardless of this, Flathead in northwestern Montana holds an almost unmeasurable amount of large Lake Superior whitefish, some approaching ten pounds.

With the collapse of the kokanee salmon population (for a variety of reasons, including competition from the introduced mysis shrimp), these whitefish make up nearly eighty percent of the biomass in Flathead Lake. There are also pretty good numbers of cutthroat and bull trout, along with a burgeoning population of lake trout.

To say that Flathead is huge is an understatement of considerable proportion. It is the largest natural body of fresh water west of the Mississippi, running twenty-eight miles long by an average of around six wide. The lake covers over two hundred square miles and is the repository of the Flathead, Swan, Whitefish, and Stillwater river drainages, an area that includes Glacier National Park, much of both the Bob Marshall and Mission Mountain wildernesses, and the Whitefish Mountains. The Missions rise way over a mile straight up along the eastern shore, and gentle hills of native grasses and pine roll off in the west. Good highways surround the lake and connect towns like Polson, Elmo, Somers, and Bigfork. State Parks for camping and access to the water are located around Flathead.

Flathead Lake in July from near Bigfork.

The lake is so big it creates its own microclimate. Terrific storms come up out of nowhere, killing the unwary boater with some regularity. Waterspouts have been reported here. In other words, this is big water—with big fish.

One of the best times to chase the noble whitefish is in early fall in the shallow-water areas of the bays. The species congregates in these areas, and if you are lucky they will be holding in twenty feet of water or less.

Using a sinking line and a leader of about six feet tapered to 3X and a Hare's Ear nymph, you probe the water from boats, which are easier and safer to fish from in Flathead than float tubes or canoes, until the whitefish are located. This is not all that difficult. Many people fish for them and you'll often see several boats working a productive spot.

I didn't really expect to catch the fish my first time out, but figured what the hell, I'll try anything once. As soon as my line hit bottom I began lifting and slowly retrieving. On the second lift

A typical Lake Superior whitefish taken from Flathead Lake.

something slammed the fly and the line began to roll off the 5-weight reel. Applying some resistance to my behavior, the whitefish soon swirled and boiled on the lake's surface. The thing looked like a miniature tarpon with big silvery scales and a similar body shape. The fish was worked to the boat but spooked and raced off again, dragging line behind it at a rapid clip.

I had to admit that these guys were fun. Netting the fish revealed maybe a four-pound specimen. I caught a number of others up to six pounds. Although I am an advocate of catch and release, according to Region I Fisheries Manager Jim Vashro, this population needs to be checked and maybe someday reduced to protect the other salmonid species in the lake. So I kept a few to fillet and sauté—a very nice, sweet-tasting fish.

No way do these whitefish offer the thrill or challenge of browns or rainbows, but for unsophisticated, steady action for sizable fish, they're a worthy quarry.

Perhaps the most challenging action at Flathead is fishing for the big lake trout in autumn. The cutts and bulls are pleasurable too, but all of this will have to wait for a bit. At the moment this intriguing, quality fishery is being threatened (as are many waters in the West) by a pernicious human encroachment and introduction of unwanted creatures. It is an ugly, serious situation.

Trout polemics one more time, with a bit of vengeance: Walleyes have their place in this world, I suppose, but not in Flathead Lake, dammit! They are now found in the lower section of the nearby Clark Fork River running below Missoula and the Bitterroot River coming into town from the south. There has been the distorted suggestion by a northwest Montana angling group (obviously not Trout Unlimited) to introduce the overgrown perch into Flathead Lake, the pristine repository of native stocks of westslope cutthroat trout and bull trout before these species make their wild way up the three forks of the Flathead River to isolated spawning grounds.

Add to this the "introduction" by uneducated or selfish fishermen of northern pike, largemouth bass, yellow perch, and others, and the threat to Montana's classy trout fishing becomes obvious. These "exotics" thrive on salmonid eggs, fry, and, in the case of northerns, trout exceeding twelve inches. The number of trout a twenty-pound pike eats in a year or the number of eggs and fry a five-pound walleye ingests in a season is significant.

Why do people want these fish in trout waters? Many anglers have moved to Montana (and to places like Idaho and Wyoming—locations experiencing similar problems) from regions (notably the Midwest) that offer excellent walleye, perch, sunfish, and northern fishing. So, these souls decide to bring a little bit of home along with them. And bait fishers have accidentally introduced such species as carp and redside shiners.

"This is not becoming a serious problem. It already *is* a serious problem," says Jim Vashro. "The illegal or accidental introduction of exotic species really impacts the existing fisheries and we have documented that throughout the state. We use introductions as a management tool, but when people introduce species themselves, they take the option away from us. It is really a Catch-22 situation."

Vashro ticked off a short list of waters already hammered by this twisted form of stocking:

• Grayling in Rogers Lake were wiped out by yellow perch in just a couple of years.

• Northern pike were illegally transplanted from Sherburne Lake, located on the east side of the Rocky Mountains, into Lonepine Reservoir in northwestern Montana in 1953. By 1957 they were swimming in Echo Lake near Kalispell. In the 1970s the pike spread swiftly throughout the western part of the state and are now found in at least fifty-six waters in the Clark Fork, Swan, Stillwater, Whitefish, and Kootenai drainages. They have recently been found in the Bitterroot and Upsata Lake in the Clearwater drainage.

• Ashley Lake has produced the current world record rainbow-cutthroat hybrid — a fish of thirty pounds. Recently two dead pike were found here.

• Upsata Lake was rehabbed in the mid-1950s to remove stunted yellow perch. The lake produced good rainbow trout fishing for twenty-nine years until the mid-1980s, when the perch reappeared and trout plants failed. The perch initially grew to over a foot but quickly stunted out to five inches. The lake was closed to fishing during 1987 while year-old fish-eating rainbows were introduced. Unfortunately, sixteen-thousand dollars worth of recovery efforts may go down the tubes because northerns showed up in 1988.

• Canyon Ferry Reservoir is the most popular fishery in the state and holds some truly large rainbows and browns. Recent fluctuations in the fishery have raised angler demands for the introduction of new species, notably walleyes. The Montana Department of Fish, Wildlife and Parks (MDFWP) is studying the situation for future management plans. But all of this may be moot because walleyes and northerns are beginning to appear, most likely as a result of illegal plantings.

• Buffalo Wallow Reservoir out on the high plains northeast of Lewistown in the Missouri Breaks used to provide superb fishing for rainbow trout in an area not noted for large trout populations.

In the 1980s yellow perch made an appearance and the rainbows all but disappeared. Stunted perch are now the order of the day here. A rehab would require draining the reservoir and losing several years of angling with little guarantee of success.

Once the exotics are in the lakes, they often quickly spread throughout the rivers, streams, and creeks, devastating a drainage with frightening speed.

This is just a sampling, a sad beggar's banquet, of the horror stories taking place not only in Montana, but throughout the trout fisheries of the West. Those who want their favorite exotic introduced into prime trout water are extremely vocal about their desires. Walleyes Unlimited, for example, has been known to make life miserable for fish and game personnel throughout Montana.

The argument against stocking walleyes is often countered by saying that browns, brooks, goldens, and in many cases rainbows are not native to Montana. To some extent there is validity to this viewpoint, but for the most part these salmonids have so firmly established themselves in rivers like the Madison or Missouri or in barren mountain lakes and streams that any initial damage that may have been done has long been compensated for by the creation of world-class, or at the very least, quality, fisheries.

Also, for the most part, species like walleye, perch, and northern pike are successful in outcompeting trout for both food sources and habitat. You really cannot have walleyes and trout hanging out in the same river.

And the bottom line is that trout species are carefully monitored and managed by fisheries biologists. There is a subtle difference between a professional with a Ph.D. in trout working a lake or stream and some clown dumping a bucket of walleyes in the Bitterroot.

"The discovery of walleyes in the Bitterroot and Clark could have disastrous implications," says Vashro. "One study indicated that if you mix walleyes with salmonids, you seriously impact the latter. Walleyes [along with squawfish] are also hurting the salmon in the Columbia River. Because of this and our own data, we adopted a ban on planting walleyes in waters west of the [Continental] Divide.

"Idaho also had a moratorium and now only plants walleyes after extensive study. They found that when walleyes were planted over there, the fish just leapfrogged beyond their plans and control. Walleyes are exceptionally predacious."

Once a trout fishery has been hammered by the introduction of exotics, rehabilitation is expensive and time-consuming.

Duck Lake, on the Blackfeet Indian Reservation located on the eastern edge of Glacier National Park, was considered one of Montana's finest trophy rainbow trout lakes from the mid-1950s through the mid-1960s. Suckers, probably used for bait, infested the lake and soon accounted for ninety percent of the fish biomass. The competition for food and habitat drove down trout size and numbers.

In 1985, the U.S. Fish and Wildlife Service (USFWS) applied rotenone, a fish poison, to a pair of shallow bays used by spawning suckers, killing thousands of the fish. Suckers now make up less than ten percent of the Duck Lake fishery, trout growth rates have doubled, and large trout are once again being seen, according to Ron Skates, a USFWS biologist. The cost was in the twenty-thousand-dollar range, and no one believes that the suckers have been eliminated from Duck Lake. They are a piscatorial time bomb waiting to explode.

Vashro estimates that reestablishing the grayling population in Rogers Lake may cost more than twenty-five thousand dollars, once again with no guarantee for success.

Obviously this is not a minor problem. Trout populations can disappear in just a few months with the introduction of a few buckets full of northerns or walleyes or perch or baitfish.

"I don't think most anglers realize the effect they have on a fishery when they empty their bait buckets into a lake at the end of a day's fishing," says Vashro. "We have to educate people as much and as quickly as possible."

Other problems caused by exotics, according to Vashro, are that they may hybridize with established species, they may carry and spread new diseases and parasites, and they may actually alter existing habitat.

The state of Montana is publicizing a three-pronged program that it hopes will curb the spread of exotic species, and this includes emphasizing to anglers that they should not move live fish or aquatic invertebrates from one body of water to another for any reason, nor should they release aquarium fish into natural waters. Finally, and most importantly in Vashro's eyes, is that anglers should report any illegal plantings they witness to the MDFWP.

"The potential for disaster from illegally introducing exotics is truly terrifying," concludes Vashro.

It is disheartening to realize that there are so many threats to fly fishing (and this does not include the wackos from Fund for Animals who would like to first ban catch and release and then all fishing), but a lot of progress in preserving and even improving the fisheries of this continent is also taking place. All is not doom and gloom, as they say, but being forewarned and armed with some information is a form of protection and power. And we all love power.

As I mentioned earlier, bull trout and cutthroats live in Flathead Lake, but many of them spend a large portion of their lives fighting the raging madness of spring runoff, poachers, and predators to reach spawning tributaries pouring into the Middle, North, and South forks of the Flathead River. Following spawning, some of these fish drop back down the tribs and rivers to rest up in the lake for the winter. There are times when the cutts rise to mayflies late in spring into early summer near shore, providing interesting fishing on drys with Green Drake overtones. Even the aloof bull trout will succumb to these insects on occasion — a rare sight, and a treat to take this trout on a dry fly.

Still, the most exciting fishing for me on Flathead Lake occurs in the fall when the big lake trout — to over twenty pounds — glowing up with spawning intensity, are spotted cruising near shore. This is streamer fishing for what amounts to very big brook trout.

You need a fourteen- to sixteen-foot flat-bottom boat for stability in the often choppy water and use as a casting platform. I don't own one of these, so my chances for this type of search-and-cast angling have been all too limited, but the few times I have worked over these fish have been a blast.

Depending on the shoreline structure, the fish will be swimming in ten feet or maybe a bit more water. Using a 7-weight, ten-foot Sink-Tip, and a large streamer—#2 and up—imitating another fish (trout, cisco, perch), the idea is to spot a lake trout, anticipate its movements, and then cast far enough ahead of the perceived course to allow the fly to sink to the bottom. Then, when the trout closes in, a few tantalizing strips will do the trick most of the time. The fish are aggressive at this stage of the life cycle and they attack a streamer with an obvious display of territorial imperative.

On an overcast day with a light swell on the lake, I spotted a large lake trout swimming casually along the rocky, boulder-strewn shore water. I cast maybe fifty feet out with enough additional line to cover the drift to the bottom. The fish kept coming, and then I jerked the fly, in this case a large Zonker. The rush and take was immediate, with the line strike on my part superfluous.

The thing just took off and ran into my backing. I could not check the fish. It just moved with determination in any direction it desired. The drag, tightened well down, seemed a minor hindrance. The mackinaw (a local name) started running every time I thought I was gaining control of the situation. The boat rocked back and forth with the swells, and with a delightful display of grace and dexterity I banged the hell out of my knees, shins, and hips as I staggered and lurched back and forth and all over the place.

There's a lot of water in the lake (no kidding), and the fish made no effort to wrap the line around a submerged boulder, so landing this guy was a matter of hanging on and waiting for him to tire. He did, and he weighed easily more than twelve pounds and I was hooked and I am really trying to find a way to save enough money to buy a boat and small motor so that I can go and fish Flathead Lake whenever the mood strikes me.

I've found that one can never practice too many addictive facets of the angling art. They are all necessary and proper.

Fort
Peck
Reservoir

*T*he salmon-colored dust kicked up into the air by the truck just hung around beneath a serious sun. The stuff did not go anywhere for the minutes I spent walking among the wiry clumps of sage and wild native grasses taking photographs.

Tracks from large birds — probably sage grouse — led off someplace in the powdered soil.

Low hills and a confusing array of rock formations in ocher, charcoal, sienna, and cooked pink rolled away in all directions. There was no sign of human habitation, just me and a few flies buzzing away in the early-June afternoon heat. Some cattle were wandering up a parched gully, oblivious to their open-rangeland future — meat on the slow hoof.

The narrow gravel road stretched off north toward the Charles M. Russell National Wildlife Refuge and massive Fort Peck Reservoir, my destination in this stretch of Missouri River country.

"What the hell," I figured in a moment of angling bravura back home a while back. "Anyone can catch trout in the western part of the state. I'm going off to cast large streamers to the northern pike of Fort Peck."

These streamlined predators exceed twenty pounds in this area and I'd heard of some sporadic, but at times quite good, fishing for the things in an isolated bay not far from Hell Creek, a name that was rapidly gaining in appropriateness the closer I came to the reservoir.

Of the many wildlife refuges located around Montana, this one

caught my attention because it is the largest and contains some
of the least-tamed land in North America.

After loading up several containers with warm, greasy-tasting
drinking water (there would be none where I was heading) and
topping off the truck's gas tank in Jordan (population 485), a few
bumpy miles behind me, I lurched out into some quite forbidding
terrain. Definitely not Sunday morning strolling material here.

The landscape scattered before me was vast, open, huge. The
country looked as though it had been shoved around by giant
earth-moving equipment in random fashion and then left to mature
in the wind, sun, rain, and staggering emptiness for eons.

But in this land of apparent nothing, a natural abundance of
wildlife exists, drawn to the life-giving liquid of Fort Peck. The
refuge is nearly 1 million acres surrounding the 189-mile-long
reservoir. Habitat varies from cottonwood river bottoms to badlands, breaks, forested coulees, marshes, and prairies.

More than two hundred species of birds have been spotted here
since the refuge was established in 1936, including large white
pelicans that drop out of the sky like giant blocks of cargo to
splash-land in quiet bays. Others include Merriam's turkeys, burrowing owls, great blue herons, Canada geese, and nesting colonies
of cormorants. Sharp-tailed grouse, Hungarian partridge, ducks,
sage grouse, and pheasant live here, too.

Large mammals wander this turf. Pronghorn antelope, elk,
white-tailed deer, and mule deer survive in fantastic isolation on
the refuge and the surrounding land. There are also Rocky Mountain bighorn sheep. Some of the less-popular residents, from a
soft human perspective, include rattlesnakes, spiders, mosquitoes,
and a number of other biting insects.

And then there is Fort Peck Reservoir itself. I do not care much
for walleye fishing in big lakes (it is too hard, and requires skills
and techniques I do not appreciate), but those who do claim that
this is super water. There are also black and white crappie, perch,
paddlefish, sturgeon, freshwater drum, channel cats, burbot,
sauger, carp, suckers, goldeye, and countless forage fish. Occasionally a rainbow or brown trout turns up at the end of someone's line.

But it was the crazed northerns that interested me, and I had excited visions of these green freshwater sharks slicing the water, tearing up the forage fish (and my streamers). Fantasies of long casts zipping out over the water toward the ravenous pike fueled my ten-hour drive from home over the Continental Divide and out onto the high plains and then winding around the isolated mountain ranges of central Montana before breaking free to sail along an empty highway through miles and miles of springtime prairie green that glows in the bright light of approaching summer.

Fish and game has always been present in eastern Montana, but the completion of Fort Peck Dam served to concentrate these populations. As much as I dislike most dams, without this one I would not have been seeking northerns that day. The dam is six miles long, and driving across the earthen structure consisting of millions and millions of cubic yards of fill feels more like crossing a natural bridge than like riding the crest of an impoundment.

During construction in the 1930s, a sizable portion of earth became saturated with water from the filling basin and drifted a quarter-mile into the reservoir, burying men and machines.

To appreciate the size of the reservoir, consider for a moment that the state of Missouri advertises 230,000 acres of fishing lakes, streams, and ponds. Fort Peck has more water than this.

Back in the truck I continued my bouncing cruise through small erosive valleys defined by bluffs littered with fantastic natural shapes. The mudstones and sandstones that dominate the geologic makeup of this region are a result of millions of years of formation; during much of that time the region was submerged beneath inland seas. The rocks here are relatively soft, and the elements have created a surreal setting of sedimentary distortion.

Dinosaur remains and fossils are literally lying in the dust. World-respected paleontologists spend good and dusty summers digging up these remains. Nests from the giant reptiles have been uncovered with embryonic dinosaurs intact within them.

Pulling onto a level spot overlooking a mud-and-sandstone delta formed where Hell Creek empties into Fort Peck, I set up camp, my labors briefly interrupted by a line of thunderstorms that boiled, flashed, and crackled overhead. Rain and hail hammered on the roof of the truck while sunlight flickered among the sage hills to the east. The tent was eventually raised, dinner cooked and eaten, and later, while I sipped a cup of coffee in the softening evening light, a flock of gulls made a raucous appearance above me, screaming for a handout. Soon giving up, they glided over a ridge bound for better pickings elsewhere.

A herd of antelope, silhouetted against the darkening sky, materialized on a nearby ridge. Planets and stars whirled above them. Bass vibrations from owls hunting the smooth air and distant howls of coyotes were the only sounds. As I looked back up Hell Creek, the land stretched out gracefully into the final glow of the day, the drainage silently hummed to its specific ancient rhythms. The *putt-putting* of a small outboard motor woke me to a warm clear dawn. Two anglers slowly trolled near the creek outlet before disappearing around a shoreline bend.

A brief hike back to the "main" road revealed that yesterday's rain had not turned the dirt and rock into impassable gumbo—a treacherous (and locally famous) amalgam that makes travel impossible until the heat of the sun cooks the mixture dry again. I was not stranded this time. The surface was already baked and small clouds of dust kicked up around my feet. Spines from small cactus glinted in the light of day.

Back at camp, I rigged up an 8-weight rod including a leader with a foot or so of forty-pound shock tippet as a hedge against the cutting effects of the northern's razor-sharp teeth. I pulled on some lightweight hip waders and shoved a small box of streamers in my hip pocket. I also looped a canteen of the lousy water around my neck as a hedge against dehydration later on.

Just ahead, a large and probably very old snapping turtle retreated into its shell at my approach. Several deer were feeding on the protein-rich grasses in the damp creek bottom.

Walking down the miniature delta, I noticed serpentine markings in the soil, indicating a snake had passed this way recently. Periodic corncob-like indentations along this path seemed to say "rattlesnake." The walk gained added dimensions of caution and curiosity, but the viper never made an appearance.

Hell Creek bubbled into the reservoir. Deer tracks were everywhere, and so were schools of minnows ranging in size from less than an inch in length to close to four—ideal food for northerns. A large fish broke the water's surface about seventy-five feet out from the combination sand-mud shoreline. A flash of movement upstream turned out to be a coyote ghosting quickly behind a pile of rocks.

I tied on a 1/0 black Woolly Bugger, tested the knot, and began working my way out into the shallows. I'd never been in quicksand before, so the first few sinking steps proved to be a terrifying revelation. I managed to push back through the stuff to the safety of the mucky beach. I had survived despite my panic.

Working down around the bay until I discovered a sandy beach that offered at least the illusion of firm footing, I cautiously waded about fifty feet out and began stripping line out to make a cast that would cover the water where I had seen the big fish surface. The light hammering onto the water was intense, but in brief moments of clarity I could see narrow channels washed out by Hell Creek. Brown-green growths of weeds paralleled the edges.

The first cast landed with a plop around eighty feet out, and the Bugger was quickly pulled beneath the surface as I worked the pattern back to me. Not quite three feet of retrieve, and a pike rolled over the fly and then sunk to the bottom with it clamped between its jaws. As soon as the pressure of the rod and line manifested itself, the northern shot off across the bay, tearing line that instantly became backing from the reel.

I was stunned by the behavior of the fish. Most pike, especially in warm water like this, put up a brief, stubborn, and occasionally splashy fight before coming to net like a whipped dog. Not so with this guy.

Hey. I realize that northerns are not bonefish, but standing up to my hips in this warm water with the temperature in the eighties, the sun blasting down, and the fish fighting like crazy

A northern pike.

. . . well, this was pretty damn good as far as I was concerned, and I didn't have to risk life and limb on a jet to get here, either.

I do not know how long the fight took, probably a few minutes, but the northern was a solid fish—ten pounds or so with deep green flanks and squarish elongated light cream spotting. Its stomach was almost copper and its back was a dark, smoky green. And the body was chunky, more like a twenty-pound fish.

I'll take a dozen more, please.

And I did, on about three dozen casts to the narrow creek channels in this bay. The fish could not be approached too closely, maybe forty feet, but anytime the Bugger landed in front of them and then did its jerky dance, the pike took—suddenly and fiercely. The largest fish was maybe fifteen pounds and the smallest about six. Excellent sport, and who cared why all of these northerns picked this small out-of-the-way bay.

The action stopped around nine-thirty and I quit and waited out the sun and the heat until evening when things picked up again,

An out-of-the-way bay with a few northerns along the southern side of Fort Peck Reservoir.

though not with such vigor. Nighttime always seems like it should be prime time for big fish like pike, but the largest I ever caught was in Ontario almost thirty years ago, when one inhaled a two-pound walleye I was trying to land one morning. We did not have a landing net, so my father took his pants off, tied the legs closed, and tried to scoop the thing up. The line broke. I cried, and my father said the fish was over thirty pounds. Most of my other big northerns (and muskies) have come early in the day, too.

Be that as it may, my father has since died (four packs of Luckies a day is living on the edge for anybody), but he would have loved this place and this fishing.

The only disappointment was my failure to catch a fish on a bendback saltwater pattern. The way the northerns hit the Buggers, I figured they would hit anything else that was large and garish, but I was wrong. No dice. In fact, if the huge fly landed too close to the pike, they spooked and dashed off to deep water.

Matching the forage-fish hatch for northern pike, I guess.

The next day I caught a few more pike, packed my gear, headed out the Hell Creek road into Jordan and then east and north toward Circle, and on through Glasgow before racing along the Hi-Line back home.

Tidy endings are nice and convenient, but this fishing in the sometimes harsh but always honest country of eastern Montana is really mostly about being able to find everything I could possibly desire from being alone outside in the undisciplined middle of apparent nothing.

Flathead Reservation Bass Lakes

*L*eeches are ugly.

God, I hate the things. The sight of the slimy, slithering suckers undulating through the water makes my skin crawl. What good are they? How a bait fisher can actually touch a leech, let alone jab the writhing piece of ooze on a hook, is a mystery to me.

For most of my confused life I never even fished with a leech pattern, that is up until a few years ago when I tried a #4 purple one on the bass that swim in the reservoirs of the Flathead Indian Reservation in western Montana. I soon discovered that large-mouth bass lose all control and self-respect when they see this slithery fly sliding through the water. Wading the marshy fringes of Kicking Horse Reservoir, I cast the leech out into the deeper water and then swam the thing in over submerged weed beds and along drop-offs. The bass hit on almost every cast from late after-noon until well after dark, when a horde of bloodthirsty mosquitoes drove me to the truck and the sanity of a good cigar and a cold beer.

In just a few hours, bass from a staggering six inches up to maybe a couple of pounds raced for the purple leech. Frequently two or three, or perhaps more, of them would charge at once, forcing me to jerk and skate the pattern away from the little guys (sometimes) so that the larger fish could strike. My acquaintance with leeches began when a friend gave me a dozen or so of the pattern tied in purple, black, brown, olive, and a sickly red. Ex-perimentation with these colors on the next visit here seemed to indicate that purple is the color of choice, with black next and brown and olive tied for third. This order also holds up when fishing for trout in large reservoirs and small ponds east of the Rockies out on the high plains. Purple looks basically black with just a touch of color for zip. The black just looks black and perhaps a bit on the drab side of the street for most rambunctious game-fish. When I fish leeches now (and it is still not very damn often), purple is the color and #2 and #4 are the sizes. The simpler the better in my constantly addled condition.

This all adds up to anomalous sport here in trout country. The Mission Mountains flank the eastern horizon with ice-scoured peaks covered, even in late summer, with extensive snowfields — true cutthroat trout country. And a number of rivers, reservoirs, and creeks hold solid populations of the cutts, along with browns, rainbows, brookies, and bull trout. Even after fishing the Ninepipe Reservoir located a few miles south for over twenty years for large-mouths, I still looked upon the Flathead Reservation as trout country. All of those peaks and acres and acres of pine forest seem to belie the presence of the bass. I mean, I fish for the species down here a couple of times each year and I still cannot convince myself that this is bass country. Bass are fun to catch, especially when they hit deer-hair poppers on the surface. Ounce for ounce, they are a stronger fish than trout. They are great sport on a fly rod, though I much prefer trout for a hundred different reasons, among which is that I hate high-powered, metal-flaked bass boats, orange jumpsuits that say "Bassmeister" all over the place, and terms like "ole bucketmouth" (reminds me of a school-teacher-turned-editor I once worked for), "hawg," and "flippin'."

Despite these notable shortcomings, I find much of interest concerning *Micropterus salmoides* (forgive the brief burst of ostentation). I was surprised to discover that the fish were introduced to the Columbia River system well before the turn of the century, having always figured the species was a relatively recent transplant dragged along by some bass-plug fanatic from Florida or somewhere else terminally hot and muggy. That the fish prefer weedy areas is no surprise, and adults will eat almost anything

*Dr. Jim Casada fishes for bass on Kicking Horse Reservoir
with the Mission Mountains in the background.*

once the water warms in late spring. This includes crayfish, scuds, frogs, other fish, and snakes. Early spring and fall are not good times to chase largemouth — the water is too cold to trigger steady feeding. They usually spawn in Montana sometime in late May or early June. Bass on spawning beds are too easy to catch. I once saw a smallmouth in the Missouri River near Yankton, South Dakota, hook itself on an olive Woolly Bugger on three straight casts, and the fish was ready for more. At times like these, leave them alone. They are too vulnerable, as are most of us. A two- or three-pound bass is a decent specimen at this latitude. Fish over five pounds are rare.

When using streamer patterns, a leader of nine feet tapered to either 4X or 5X does the trick. Anything stouter is not required — the bass do not grow that big. The increase in natural swimming action — and this is crucial with leeches — more than offsets the occasional break-off caused by a feisty fish resisting a light tippet.

I use a 5-weight, which offers a suitable balance between casting distance and sporting qualities. In the shallows, the weight of the streamers is sufficient to reach the bottom. In deeper water a six-foot, then around drop-offs a ten-foot, Sink-Tip is appropriate. The bigger bass hang out around these shelves, racing up to swallow an unwary minnow or two. I always look for these locations and often discover them in low-light conditions when a step forward fills my hip waders, a sensation that ranks right up there with the best life has to offer the angler.

The quality of the bass fishing on the Reservation is quite high and likely to stay so based on the management plans of the Confederated Salish and Kootenai Tribes. Although many Reservation waters, including the rivers and high mountain lakes, are strictly for various trout species, a number of the reservoirs and even a few potholes are being managed, with stable populations of bass a priority.

"You wouldn't think the bass would do well in our climate, but they do remarkably well," says tribal fisheries manager Joe DosSantos. "Many of our [tribal] members and plenty of other anglers really enjoy fishing for the species. We think that is great, especially since we are able to offer them such a fine resource and we plan to keep improving on what we have."

This and many other progressive aspects of the tribes' fishery management program are for fly fishers, to say the least, exciting. Within a decade the Flathead Reservation will probably boast, in addition to the largemouth, pristine high-mountain-lake fishing for native westslope cutthroat trout (by this I mean better than the wonderful action that already exists), quality brown and rainbow trout fishing in several rivers (and below Kerr Dam in the main stem of the Flathead River in the next century when the tribes take over operation of the dam from Montana Power Company), trophy lake trout in Flathead Lake, and a stable population of bull trout and large northern pike in the lower stretches of the Flathead River. Take your pick. The future seems bright on the Reservation compared to many waters on state and federal land that are rapidly being destroyed by clear-cutting, mining, development, and oil and gas exploration. At least there will be fishing left on the Reservations of Montana in the twenty-first century (rumors of outrageous and very off-limits trophy rainbow trout activity on the Crow Reservation float through Whitefish at times).

While leeches and other streamers catch bass, the most fun is driving largemouths nuts with deer-hair poppers on the surface. These bulky contraptions have a flat or dish-shaped face that pops and bubbles the water surface when they are retrieved with stops and starts and jerks. In the evening as the sun goes down (sounds of a 1968-version Lou Rawls crooning some cocktail jazz wafts across the reservoir, providing suitable background for what is about to transpire), casting a popper dyed to resemble a frog or mouse or downed Cessna can be as much fun as sex (pretty close, anyway, and without many of the complications). The things are difficult to cast if there is any wind about. A fairly stiff 6-weight with weight-forward line is a choice of reason and taste with shades of function.

Wing the popper into some shoreline reeds. Let it sit for a minute (really). Waiting for sixty seconds while the water quiets down, all the time secure in the belief that a big bass is staring up at the floating phony is high drama. Getting there is half the fun. Twitch the bugger. Often a bass will smash it right there. If not, start to pulse the bug back to you. The more racket you make, the better. These fish are not shy. They are *aggressive*. One time I did this and the next moment a fast approaching V-wake appeared behind my imitation frog. The back of a bass broke water. A largemouth devoured the deer hair. All hell broke loose. This took three seconds. The fish rose up on its tail and waggled back and forth. There was no doubt in my mind that it was not happy with life at that moment. I could see clearly the fake frog hooked in the corner of the large mouth. That bass jumped and ran all over the place, eventually winding up tangled around some weeds. I cautiously approached as I reeled in the thrumming line, certain that break-off time was at hand. Looking down on the clumped reeds, I saw the bass trying to swim off to a better land. I scooped it up in the net just as the leader popped. A two-pounder that fought like four.

"That was fun," I said out loud to myself and cast away like a happy child in the dwindling light, taking plenty of other largemouth before darkness and the mosquito crowd called a halt to the proceedings. I'm glad there is action like this in Montana. Too much of my youth was spent chasing bass in Illinois and southern Wisconsin farm ponds to ever cleanse that addiction from my system.

Where wading the shoreline of Kicking Horse is as productive as any method of fishing, a float tube works far better on Ninepipe. The water drops off quickly in many areas of this reservoir, making wading a short-lived, difficult proposition. The same tactics that take bass on Kicking Horse work here. The purple leeches still spin their ugly voodoo and the poppers still provoke violent responses from the reed beds. The only difference is that the largemouths run a little larger in Ninepipe. Where they average about one pound in Kicking Horse, the median here is maybe one and a half pounds. Ninepipe is eighteen hundred acres when full, compared to eight hundred acres. Both places have perch and sunfish. The latter can kill a slow hour if you use little red or yellow cork-bodied poppers. Sunfish are pretty things, and those that approach a half-pound in weight put up spirited resistance.

The last time I fished Kicking Horse was during the dog days of summer. Trout streams were low and unfishable. The lakes were so warm that the trout had dropped down to cold-water holes to wait out the heat. The temperature was way into the nineties and the sky was hazy. Not exactly ideal conditions, but I figured that maybe a bass or two would cooperate, so I made the hour-plus drive south from home, tied on a leech, and cast it upon the water. I just let the whole mess sink to the bottom, content to enjoy the cool water. It was too hot for waders. I wished I was up in the Missions sliding down a patch of snow or passed out on a cool ridge somewhere, but I wasn't.

Line began running off the reel and I automatically lifted the rod tip. A big, dumb bass immediately began to tear up the lake's surface. Astonishment reigned. The fish kept running and jumping. I held on, finally gaining back line when the largemouth tired.

The sight of my white legs triggered another run. Understandably. I cranked the fish back to shore. Definitely over two pounds. Possibly three.

The bass had sucked in the leech off the bottom while I was lost in space somewhere.

I'll take brain-dead angling anywhere I can find it.

Lower-
Elevation
Mountain
Lakes

Nature's intricacies are rarely understood by the casual observer or by me, and I spend a good deal of time examining the world as it applies to fly fishing. Certainly not to the extent of Swisher, Richards, or Schwiebert, but I know a little bit, like the difference between a caddis and a small stonefly, or when trout are taking emergers and not duns. The intricate aspects of the pursuit.

Aside from the many pleasures associated with lakes and streams, unspoiled country, good friends, and of course the trout themselves, one of the overriding attractions of fly fishing is the concentric nature of the acquisition of angling knowledge and experience. The more I learn the more I realize how little I know.

Not being able to understand everything about anything used to drive me crazy. Not any more. I don't care. The fact that I'll never absorb more than a mere touch of the reality that is fly fishing is comforting. A burden is gone. Since I can't possibly know it all, anything I figure out on the water is a bonus, a gift from somewhere above.

Such is the case when I'm fishing lower-elevation lakes in northwest Montana. There are hundreds of them, often surrounded by dense pine forest or moist meadows of deep grass with small groves of aspen here and there. Even the most obscure small range of hills has a few lakes. Look at any forest service map and you'll locate them. Rainbows, cutthroats, and brookies swim in these waters. I've spent enough time on these lakes to become fairly adept at taking fish. When I work at the process, the action is steady, and often good, for large trout.

Landing a typical low-elevation northwest Montana lake rainbow.

These lakes (and most others located in temperate latitudes) have well-defined cycles, times when certain layers of even-temperature water are found at specific depths. Such as cold on the bottom and warm on top, to be wildly simplistic. Without understanding the movements of these layers, catching trout can be tough, which is characterizing the situation mildly.

On a small body of water not far from home, a place I often go to when I'm done writing for the day, the fishing can be entertaining for rainbows up to two feet. This lake is one of the very few that is catch and release in the Flathead Valley. Despite this, the meat-mongers nail it with ruthless intent, especially the snowmobile crowd in the dead of winter, when enforcement officials are occupied with other projects.

Even with this greedy predation the lake manages to maintain a decent population of trout. An abundance of damsel and dragonflies, caddis, mayflies, midges, flying ants, and moths is responsible for this phenomenon. The water is extremely clear and quite cold, even in July. The bottom is covered with rich aquatic plant growth. Clumps of lily pads and patches of duckweed thrive in small bays.

Early in the year, just after ice-out, I would fish the depths initially, thinking the trout would be down below in the warmer water waiting for the spring sun to warm the surface. I rarely touched fish. This and other misconceptions held forth with seasonal regularity until I began to explore the mysteries of turnover. Up until several years ago most of my time was spent working moving water. Flat water seemed boring. I was wrong, obviously. So what's new? I still believe that democracy and not capitalism is the driving force in this country.

At any rate, the sight of dozens of trout feeding aggressively on the surface of this lake, only recently free of ice, piqued my curiosity. Had the surface already warmed to such an extent that it now offered the optimum temperature zone, or were the fish here because of light intensity?

The answer, while involving fairly complex hydrological movements, is not exceptionally complicated. The lake has simply "turned over." In other words, the various layers of water existing at different temperatures are no longer stratified but are now mixed together (lengthening days and increased light intensity from the sun will layer the water once again, this time in somewhat reverse order, with cooler temperatures found near the lake's bottom). The end result is that the entire body of water is relatively uniform in temperature, eliminating the need for trout to hold in the most oxygen-rich layer. The amount of suspended oxygen available throughout the lake is virtually constant; therefore, other variables (mainly where food sources are most abundant) now influence the trout's behavior. The lake has essentially become a one-level system, though not for long. The fish will be concentrated in a level of water at the surface. They won't be here long, maybe a few weeks at most. After this, it is time to begin working the depths where the trout are now hiding from the heat and bright light, except during dawn and dusk and periods of overcast. Got to have those exceptions to keep life interesting.

Casting streamers, nymphs, and even wet flies toward shore and swimming them back in darting retrieves normally entices trout, which will be working around piles of logs, boulders, or right next to shore. I've taken three good trout from one downed log on three straight casts, and this despite the racket each fish made when it fought. They feed with a determination that is unchecked early in the year.

Lakes, ponds, and reservoirs are stratified into three layers. The top one is called the *epilimnion* and is the level warmed by the sun. The bottom layer, or *hypolimnion,* is located far enough below the surface so that the sun has little if any effect on it. The middle layer, or *thermocline,* is a transitional zone of fairly swift temperature change. Temperature changes are often a half-degree per foot or more. Trout are found in this zone during the warmer months because this is a region that contains their preferred temperature level.

Once summertime water conditions arrive, working a dry on the surface from a float tube is not a productive endeavor. On many of these lakes trout will be rising periodically and the temptation is to cast near a riseform. Unless the lake is alive with working fish, there are better methods to use. The best and most difficult is to use at least a ten-foot Sink-Tip line and crawl a nymph along the bottom or just above the plant growth. In deep lakes a full-sink line is needed. Obviously, retrieving and casting this type of setup is labor intensive, but the routine produces fish. Often the take comes as you bring the nymph back up toward you. The pattern travels through prime-time water where the trout are holding, and the motion imitates the behavior of many aquatic insects as they struggle to the surface. A strike from a twenty-inch rainbow while you have perhaps nine feet of leader and five feet of line out virtually right below your fins manifests certain innate elements of high drama. I've had trout strike and then bounce off my fins, then race wildly through and around my legs — a terrible mess that predictably ends in a break-off and some creative obscenity-stringing.

Any lake that has those electric blue damsels flying around is a prime candidate for damsel nymphing. There are a number of fine patterns, but I prefer Kaufmann's or the Biggs Special (aka Sheep Creek). Both outfish other ties, especially when pulled up through the water column with a varying, undulating retrieve. The main difficulty is setting the hook. Sinking lines acquire a healthy amount of belly in them as they drop down below, and even when they are worked rapidly. Both the line hand and the rod are required to strike the trout. The fish strike aggressively, but most separations occur because the slack is not swiftly dealt with.

One other tactic that works with decadent consistency is to cast an imitation of a downed dragonfly out onto the surface. Then twitch the ungainly thing to create the illusion (all of fly fishing flirts with illusion on a more or less constant basis) of struggle, as if a real one were trapped in the surface film. You may have to do this for some minutes. What the hell? Time's on your side. Touch off a cheap cigar and keep on twitchin'. When the take comes, and it will, the investment in minutes will prove worthwhile. A big trout will crunch the thing with a racket reminiscent of a canoe capsizing. This is truly wonderful sport for the sincerely lazy among us. I'm as good as anyone in the world at this aspect of fly fishing.

At times when the fish are working on the surface, anticipation and careful casting are prerequisites to success. Trout seem to work in groups up and down a shoreline. In float tubes, two anglers are better than one. Spread apart; the pair can alert each other to approaching fish, allowing each to cast well out ahead of the working trout. In clear water during calm-water feeding periods, stealth is absolutely necessary. Even a marginally noisy cast will scare off the fish.

I often employ another approach. Casting from a large downed larch at a lake located in the Swan Range south of my home is excellent sport in a contemplative way.

I rig up a 4-weight with a twelve-foot leader and a #16 dark caddis of some sort, then wing the thing fifty feet or so out on the lake. Next, I light a cigar and sip a cool beverage while waiting for the fast westslope cutthroats to cruise my way, and they never fail to do so.

Walking out on the log disturbs the water and spooks any nearby trout, but after a bit the fish return. The sippings that tip off the head-and-tail rises of the cutthroat are audible from the length of a football field in the stillness. Ideally, the lake's surface is mirror smooth, reflecting the forest and sky. A few swirls are visible out in the middle. Perhaps a raven voices an opinion from the top of a snag. Water from a tiny feeder creek bubbles away and the cutthroat work closer.

At one hundred feet and closing I send the fly in their direction as softly as possible. I feel like an actor in *Run Silent, Run Deep*. When the trout are within ten feet or so I just barely twitch the fly—an attention-getter of sorts. No mad trout rushes, but I'm confident that the fish have spotted the caddis. In a few seconds a swirl marked by a head, back, and tail fin porpoise where the caddis once floated. A light set and a brief splashing confrontation end with a dark-backed cutthroat thrashing alongside the old larch. Wonderful, wild trout. They are amazing to me, living in this timbered country that is vanishing at a frightening rate from rapacious logging. Sharp mountain peaks rise above. The valley and another range float off toward the far horizon. The trout have moved on downshore and are now congregated about a cluster of downed lodgepole, feeding casually among the cover.

A soft blast of cool air blows over me as it follows the drainage corridor. I take a sip from my drink and a puff on my cigar, then dry the caddis and cast the line out again in anticipation of the next wave of trout.

Not extremely challenging angling. Just way out there serene, totally relaxed, without thought or worry.

I could do this forever.

Clark
Canyon
Reservoir

When you do not really know a piece of water, taking that first decent trout of the day is always something of a surprise if not actually a revelation. Paddling my float tube from the submerged roadway at the south end of the Clark Canyon Reservoir over to the clumps of dead brush took a few minutes. Spent midges covered the surface of the milky, jade-colored water. I cast a Kaufmann damsel nymph and, as is usual for me, I made a dozen or so more casts and accompanying retrieves before I could relax and settle into a "predatory" rhythm.

Working nymphs with Sink-Tip lines takes concentration to be more than marginally successful. Not that this is Bobby Fischer chess-match brainwork, but the more things I manage to do correctly, the higher the odds of turning a trout. Maintaining constant control of the line with one hand while keeping the rod tip in position to strike is important. I like the tip just above the water and angled slightly to one side of the line. Keeping the float tube aimed in the direction of the cast can help, too. Striking a trout over your shoulder may look flashy in a toreador sort of way, but is far from efficient from a strike-to-netted-fish perspective.

One of my casts managed to land a damsel nymph right in the center of a narrow lane between a pile of dead branches. The fly sank for a bit and then began its up-and-down course back to the tube. On the third series of strips and hesitations the rod was nearly jerked from my hands. Pulling back on the line brought a large rainbow rocketing out of the water, and then the fish ran back and forth, toward me, then behind me, and leaped again. This was followed by some good old-fashioned deep-water holding. The fish was difficult to move. Finally it came up and bashed around the surface before coming to my net, which it filled with ease. Small net but a nice fish of over twenty inches. My confidence grew, and by fishing determinedly I took three more rainbows and one brown before paddling back in the afternoon surf to my truck for lunch.

All of my fish that day were over twenty inches, and that translated to, by far, my best day here, but I know people who have taken more and larger fish when the conditions were propitious.

Clark Canyon can be quite good, and the fishery there survives despite obscene levels of drawdown caused by several years of low precipitation and the ensuing vicious attentions of meat-fishers. The reservoir is considered by many veteran (it's a war out there, in case you have not looked lately) anglers to have some of the best lake fishing for trout in Montana. Rainbows and browns of several pounds are taken with some regularity in this impoundment that will exceed six thousand acres on those rare occasions when it is full.

The best concentration of fish is at the southeast end, where the Red Rock River empties into the lake. An abandoned, crumbling paved road leads into the lake and you park your vehicle where the road ends and the lake starts. (Stay away from the shoulder or you'll get your rig seriously stuck in the muck and wet gravel.)

Working submerged copses of willows from a float tube with nymphs is the most popular and successful method of fishing this water. Casting 7-weight intermediate lines fifty to sixty feet with a nine-foot 7-weight rod, letting them sink for fifteen seconds, making a short strip and allowing this to rest for a count of seven, and finally making two more slow short strips often triggers strikes in the clear blue-green water. Definitely, fish out the cast. Many takes will come surprisingly close to your tube. Guide Tim Tollett showed me this retrieve, and with slight variations in pace it takes fish for me throughout the state. This is a basic, proven still-water method.

An intermediate line works, but I prefer Sink-Tips. Both six- and ten-foot lines will take fish, but the longer one seems to reach more trout and also presents a better line profile that gives the pattern, particularly damsel nymphs, a much better illusion of life. The Sink-Tips are also less labor-intensive when it comes to picking them up out of the water.

On calm days the fish are quite spooky, so leaders up to twelve feet and down to 5X are often needed to make delicate presentations to feeding trout. The small tippets can be sporting, especially so when a strong trout manages to run through a bunch of aquatic spinach that wraps around the line, greatly increasing the drag. Break-offs are not unheard of at this juncture.

Located twenty miles south of Dillon on Highway I-15, Clark Canyon lies out in open country, rolling treeless hills that slope down to the shoreline. Because of this terrain, wind is an element that deserves an angler's attention and respect.

One morning I was peacefully casting to gulping trout on a mirrorlike water surface, and fifteen minutes later I was being buffeted amid rolling whitecaps that spilled over the back of my tube. At times like these the fishing can be entertaining, but for safety's sake it is prudent to head into shore.

Some of the better patterns include the Biggs Special (Sheep Creek) #8 to #10, the Prince, the Flashback in #12 to #16, and leech patterns in #2 to #8. Buggers and olive Zonkers are not bad, either. Olive scuds should be included in any selection. Drys would include *Callibaetis,* midges, damselflies, ants, and hoppers in the heat of summer.

On one noteworthy trip with Tollett, a carp over twelve pounds hammered one of his nymphs and streaked off into the depths. We both thought the fish was a huge brown, but when the angry creature was brought up to our tubes we had a good, if slightly incredulous, laugh. Trophy trash fishing, big time in Montana.

Ice-out is usually in mid-April, and the fishing begins with leeches and dragon and damsel nymphs. By mid- to late June *Callibaetis* and midges (large sizes of #12 to #14) appear. July to August is the time for damsels. In September and October much of the

*Tim Tollett fishes Clark Canyon Reservoir: He's playing a
large fish that hit a nymph.*

action shifts back to *Callibaetis* and midges. Good, crafty fish can
be taken by working the numerous cold-water spring areas. Large
streamers always produce, but when the trout are gulping on top,
drys are more fun, obviously. Watching a large fish inhale tiny
insects, jaws agape, perhaps not more than twenty feet distant,
makes for shaky hands.

   If you desire a change of pace or need a break from the fierce
winds of Clark Canyon Reservoir, the serene pace of Poindexter
Slough is the ideal solution. Serene even though I-15 passes right
over prime water. Located just a couple of miles south from Dillon,
this spring-fed creek wanders through fields of hay, its banks
covered with willows. The slough is filled with weed beds that
wave slowly back and forth in the crystal-clear water. The gravel
bottom, along with the rainbows and browns that discriminatingly
sip drys in the lanes between the aquatic growth, are clearly visible
from above through the glasslike surface of the flow. These gravel

runs are only a few feet deep, but there are pockets and holes much deeper. They'll "float your hat," as the old saying goes.

Long leaders, small tippets, and tiny drys are the weapons of choice here for trout that average around twelve inches but will run larger.

This is classic spring-creek angling. Targeting a feeding fish, making a careful stalk along the bank, and then very cautiously presenting your fly is the only method that produces consistently. Even then, the fishing is demanding but made all the more enjoyable when a skillful presentation (a feat I accomplish with studied rarity) results in a tricked trout.

If there is one stream in Montana where I would dare, and wish, to bring out my treasured seven-and-a-half-foot 3-weight bamboo rod, Poindexter is that place. Twelve-foot leaders and tippets tapered down to 7X are common fare here. You can easily spend fifteen minutes working your way close to a wary fish and then making what you think is a perfect cast, only to have the finicky guy dash under a clump of weeds.

In April and May, and again from September through October, *Baetis* hatch in good numbers. Pale morning duns and caddis hold sway in July and August.

Both drys and nymphs, cast quartering well upstream from working fish and then drifted directly into the feeding lane, turn the difficult trick. These trout see a lot of flies during the course of the season, so the angling is tough. This is just another course for those majoring in the fly fishing program for world-class trout maniacs at the University of Dillon-Area.

One September, while returning from fishing Yellowstone Park, I decided to try Clark Canyon. I headed to Dillon over some back roads that crossed both the Gravelly and Snowcrest mountains. The summertime crush of visitors was over. The diminished intensity from their departure was palpable. The climate felt peaceful, calm. Fall colors were starting to show in the undergrowth, and aspen leaves rustled dryly at the slightest suggestion of a breeze. A light wind was blowing as I rigged up at the reservoir.

The water felt cool, even through neoprene waders. I'd tied on

a Biggs Special. Tollett mentioned once that he believed the tie
to be the best pattern around for fishing western lakes and reservoirs. Subsequent experimentation on my part made me a believer.
No matter where I cast the thing, it always produces, often much
better than leeches, Buggers, Zonkers, or damsel imitations. The
Biggs looks sparse dry, but in the water it takes on a life of unexpected dimensions; a synergy of water and materials occurs.

I returned to the clumps of brush and cast tight to the over-
hanging limbs. Second cast, first strip, and the fly was smashed.
Something big ran for the cover of the dead stuff. I just barely
managed to check whatever it was by pulling back and up with
the rod, all the time paddling furiously backward. The fish then
streaked off to my left for the safety of depth. I turned in this
direction. The trout (I did wonder if this was a big carp) ran back
and forth and dogged my every attempt to turn it. After some
minutes of pulling and trying to horse the thing (3X tippet makes
for confidence in open water), I saw the flash of trout. Large,
dark, and golden, it was huge. The brown ran from the sight of
my legs and flippers. Line zipped off the reel. Some more tug-of-
war action before the trout could be pulled, but not dragged, to
me. My net opening is eighteen inches, and the brown was six
inches, at least, beyond that. He would not fit. Clamping the rod
with the tube's Velcro holders, I grabbed the fish behind the head,
sort of, and pried the Biggs loose from a toothy jaw with forceps.
The curved kype was already well formed. The fish worked free
of my hand and sank from sight.

That was enough for me. Quit while you are ahead. Dark clouds
were riding up from the north. The air was cold and the smell
of coming snow was on the wind. Time to drive home. Thoughts
of the big brown would help pass the drive time. I was satisfied.

Georgetown Lake

Damsels!

*L*et's get to the heart of the matter. The first time I laid eyes on Georgetown Lake, somewhere back in the overbright early seventies, I was unimpressed. The lake reminded me of some crazed, resort-ridden, tourist-infested, ski-boat-ravaged lake of the hot midsummers of my northern Wisconsin youth.

In short, the place did absolutely nothing for me. And when I finally fished the place recently with my good friend John Talia, my opinion of the lake did not improve.

John is a good fly fisher, and occasionally I catch nice trout. On this outing two of the brook trout I took were just barely bigger than the damselfly nymph I was using — real wall-hangers — and a third peaked out at around eight inches. John nailed a ten-incher through a bit of angling artifice (he changed patterns), skill, and the brute force of a 7-weight rod in calm water.

"Worst fishing I've ever seen here. The worst," said John around mouthfuls of French fries, cheeseburger, and gulps of margaritas. "Usually you'll take at least a couple of sixteen-inchers and maybe a good rainbow down there."

"Down there" was along the east shoreline that parallels Highway 1. There were still two other tubers and a couple of boats out. I scanned the lake, taking in the numerous resort homes, a large marina, more boats, and gentle tree-covered hills.

The lake, located at over six thousand feet above sea level, covers more than three thousand acres. It is fertile, as the lush weed growth covering the bottom indicates. Georgetown rests in a large

75

hole (or valley) just west of the Flint Range, southwest of the Ana-
conda Pintlar Wilderness, and a few air miles east of the Sapphire
Mountains. It takes about an hour or so to get to the water from
either Butte or Missoula.

Serious fly fishers come here for the brook and rainbow trout
that work the many large bays for forage fish, damsels, and other
aquatic nymphs. Early in the cold nastiness of spring and again
in the often-similar conditions of autumn are considered prime
times for good fish. When you find the level the fish are working
at and manage the proper retrieve, the fishing can be "Fantastic,"
or so I was told. Actually, I've seen photographs of very fine trout
that John's taken from here, so this is not by any stretch a western
Montana goose chase honking away in the pine-scented breeze.

Another barrier, for me at least, is that Georgetown (and it certainly is not alone in this problem) attracts hordes of "sportsmen"
each spring just after ice-out (usually around May 10) on tributaries where these gentle souls club to death thousands of spawning
rainbows as they try and make their way up the little creeks. The
skill, intricate behavior, high drama, and moral implications of
this absurdity deserve the literary attentions of John Updike.

The event is now known locally as the "late great spawning
slaughter." It has attracted an elite crew that even includes chil-
dren and those in wheelchairs to places like Emily Spring for de-
cidedly easy pickings. Taking trout here has been described as
"fishing in a bathtub."

The massacre has led to closure of certain areas of the lake until
early summer, and the chaos may be having a gradual impact on
the genetic makeup of the rainbows. Numbers and average size
may be declining. And you wonder why meat hunters are giving
our pursuit a bad name.

Indeed, on our outing we watched two guys masquerading as
fly fishers slinging treble hooks and a lot of weight over cruising
trout near shore. This is sophisticated action at its finest. Snagging
is as natural to some in Montana as is cutting down anything that
grows with a chainsaw. "It's a God-given right, don't ya know."

Adding to the general excitement is the fact that there are also good numbers of kokanee salmon that are pushovers for trolled strips of sheet metal and treble hooks. A few bull trout and suckers swim here, too.

As one angler said casually that unproductive day as he paddled by in his battered float tube, "It took me awhile to figure the lake out, but now that I've got things down cold, I hit fish every time out." And at least on this day he put John and me to shame, taking over a dozen fish while we practiced the high art of futility. Sort of a Babe Ruth to John's Marc Hill and my Moe Thacker gig, but then, you had to be there.

It was a pretty day, but I doubted then that I'd ever come back. I mean, where would you rather fish—at a midwestern resort pond or way back in the northern Rockies somewhere catching beautifully colored native westslope cutthroat trout on drys at an unknown lake below an ice-blasted, extreme mountain cirque?

The answer for me was obvious. So long Georgetown. So John and I bounced back over the shining Sapphires down wonderfully unlogged (so far) Skalkaho Pass listening to old Doors songs. It was a beautiful day (we may have listened to that tape, also), a scenic drive, and despite the poor fishing, an enjoyable adventure.

Understanding something about anything in life is more often than not a case of a harmonious collision between luck and exasperated experimentation.

Such was the case with Georgetown Lake (along with damselflies) in my hit-or-miss angling learning curve. I eventually gave in to my dwindling sense of fair play and overriding curiosity, returning to Georgetown in late September. The brookies were beginning to approach spawning velocity, and the damsels were still flying electric blue or wriggling dull olive and bulky in the clear water. The fishing was "Fantastic!" and I tagged some brookies to at least sixteen inches, maybe a touch larger. Things change and this is true big time in mountain lakes. Georgetown is no exception, but one thing I know is that I'll always carry plenty of damsel nymphs.

Working damselfly (Odonata) nymphs along shorelines and in among weed beds during the height of summer seemed to be the appropriate method—one that normally proved quite effective in taking good numbers of often sizable trout with consistency.

The discovery that fishing the nymphs would take trout from ice-out through freeze-up on lakes and reservoirs in Montana (and other parts of the country) was a surprise of near epic proportions in my sedate existence.

A small lake lying in a forest of larch not far from home in northwest Montana was the scene of this embryonic revelation. The similarities between this pond and Georgetown—in clarity, depth, and altitude—were significant. A few days after the water opened up found me working the shoreline from a float tube with a variety of nymphs designed to imitate the abundant caddisfly population. When the insects began rising from the lake in swarms and the few rising trout ignored all of the dry patterns I cast, frustration led me to my fly boxes.

This lake had always yielded rainbows of size and distinction on damsel nymphs during July and August, but would these patterns work in early April—the time of transition between winter and spring in the northern Rockies? After a long, dark winter devoid of the frenzied tug of a good trout, I would find out.

An olive Kaufmann's Marabou Damsel tied to the end of a nine-foot leader tapered to 4X that was attached to a Teeny sinking-tip line and cast toward shore took fish immediately. Crawling the pattern along the bottom as slowly as possible produced a rainbow of eighteen inches. The trout slammed the nymph and started running directly toward the float tube and my fins, which were now furiously paddling away from the impending entanglement.

I eventually landed and released the rainbow. The fly line was finally unwound from my legs and the tube. And some new questions surfaced in a dazed angling mind. Chief among them were: Do trout feed on damsels with regularity in the spring? The fall? What behavior in the species triggers this feeding? What retrieves work best? And what patterns work best?

Tom Weaver, a fisheries biologist for the Montana Department of Fish, Wildlife and Parks, provided most of the answers. The information applies to any body of water that holds damselflies and, to a lesser extent, dragonflies.

"Fish root for the nymphs early in the year. They kick them loose from plant stems and the bottoms," said Weaver. "And, to some extent, they are keyed into them along the bottom all of the time."

Most of us are familiar with the electric blue, slender-bodied damsels that cruise just above the surface of a lake, often in great numbers. And many of us have seen the windrows of the dead insects piled up along shore, against downed trees, or along weed beds, usually washed up by wind-driven wave action. The temptation is to fish a dry pattern of the insect, and many attractive and inventive imitations are on the market. Unfortunately, these creative ties are largely ineffective, particularly when compared to the results garnered by nymphal patterns.

The reasons for this are relatively straightforward.

The majority of the damselfly's life is spent in a series of naiad, or nymphal, stages. And since the insect in various stages is moving about the entire year, trout have learned to feed on them more or less constantly. (The old "availability of a food source" syndrome.) These ugly creatures bear only passing resemblance to the beautiful airborne stages. The stout, chunky nymph is usually gray, greenish, or similarly subdued in color. The body may be smooth, or rough and bearing small spines. It is often covered with a growth of filamentous algae or debris. The naiads are commonly found on submerged vegetation and the bottoms of reservoirs, ponds, lake shallows, and in quiet areas of rivers and streams.

A one-year life cycle is the norm, with substantial variation among species. There is often more than one generation per year, but at the other end of the damsel spectrum some of the larger members may require more than four years to complete a life cycle. Much of this time is spent crawling along the bottom of the habitat or up and down plant stems.

Odonata nymphs may be roughly classified into climbers, sprawlers, and burrowers. The first two types attract the most attention from trout. Most of the sprawlers are long-legged, slow-moving, dull-colored insects that occur on a variety of types of lake bottoms.

Damselfly nymphs are most vulnerable to trout at two key times in their lives: when feeding and when rising to the surface to hatch.

Although all odonate nymphs are carnivorous, feeding methods vary. Some species carefully stalk their prey. Many of the burrowing forms remain motionless, waiting for food to come within reach. These may remain motionless for days at a time, which explains why this type of damselfly nymph is not high on a trout's list of things to see and eat.

Very large nymphs can often seize prey up to twenty-five millimeters (nearly one inch) away through a combination of labium (the liplike structure of the nymph) action and a quick forward-lurching movement.

While all of this information seems somewhat pedestrian in nature, it is the key to enticing trout to strike a nymphal imitation.

Fishing damselfly nymphs successfully, especially early and late in the season, requires that the angler first get the imitation to the bottom and then carefully crawl the nymph back to him. A weighted pattern and a Sink-Tip line are prerequisites for taking fish. If repeated retrieves fail to turn a fish, the lurching, aggressive feeding action should be imitated.

Even when trout have been rising and slashing all around me as they fed on mayflies and caddis, if I am able to display a modicum of self-control and manage to carefully work the bottom with a damselfly nymph, I normally catch fish, and they are often larger on average than those taken on top.

"Once they key into them [the bottom-dwelling nymphs], the trout really feed on them," adds Weaver. "They do act the same way as a cold-blooded animal. In cold water they are in low gear and in warm water high gear, so the action increases with water temperature."

That the damselfly nymphs are large and relatively easy to spot makes them a more attractive target, as far as trout are concerned, than the quickly darting damselflies flying above a lake's surface.

While these techniques work especially well in the spring and fall and do take fish in the summer, the best warm-weather approach mimics the damsels as they work to the surface and crawl out on emergent aquatic vegetation or fixed objects. Most odonates emerge in the early morning or late afternoon with a very few making the move during midday or during darkness.

"The prehatch ritual often includes distinct swimming movements that consist of two, three, or four trips from the bottom to surface and back down again before they are able to break the surface film and get into the air to dry off," said Weaver. "This is a perilous existence and the trout really hammer them at this time."

Imitating this motion is not difficult, and I have had the best results using a fairly long leader (twelve feet) tapered to no more than 3X. Any less and the hard takes of the trout will snap the tippet. Much larger and the pattern is exposed as a fake. The length allows for good sinking and a natural motion of the imitation.

Weighted damselfly nymphs cast forty to fifty feet and allowed to sink to the bottom are then stripped in short (two- to four-inch) retrieves back to the angler. These are done in a series until the nymph reaches the surface. The sequence is something of an acquired rhythm that will vary slightly from lake to lake. A group of three or four strips followed by a brief rest (a couple of seconds) and then a resumption of the retrieve has proved itself over time for me. Experimentation in different localities will turn up the proper sequence for them.

As for the best patterns, at least in my experience there do not seem to be any—fished properly, they all work. I've had consistent results with Kaufmann's pattern, along with those designed by A. K. Best, Janssen, and Whitlock. I've also fished olive Woolly Worms, Zug Bugs, and Prince nymphs in a damsel manner and taken trout who were feeding on the aquatic form.

A fairly stiff rod of about 6-weight and nine feet provides sufficient lifting action to eliminate much of the casting labor without destroying the joy and sport of presentation and the playing of a twelve- to fifteen-inch trout. The setup will also handle bigger fish that happen along.

As with any new technique (and most other aspects of life), I am

John Talia fishes for brookies on Georgetown Lake.

a confirmed skeptic until shown otherwise. The notion that working damselfly nymphs in mid-November would take trout seemed
farfetched until one afternoon last autumn.

   Fishing a small lake with Whitlock's pattern and carefully crawling the thing slowly along the bottom, turned up four rainbows
up to twenty inches in length for me. All of this took place as
a winter storm rolled in from the northwest. At the end of the
outing there were several inches of snow on the logging road where
my truck was parked. The storm continued for another twelve
hours and ended that year's fishing, but learning a little about
the versatility of the damselfly nymph was for me one of a very
pleasant season's highlights.

   So one October day I cast damsel nymphs with the ten-foot Sink-
Tip and crawled them just above the weed growth, sometimes
hanging up in stuff. The brook trout came out of the cover,
slashing at the pattern and deep-water running until they tired
and came to me to be netted.

Brookies in spawning dress are just flat-out gorgeous fish. Golden trout have nothing on these guys.

When I mentioned this outing to John, he laughed and added, "Dammit! I knew we'd just had a bad day. Oh, I wish I'd been there."

Thinking about Georgetown now I find myself looking at the lake with a different perspective. What was once a bunch of water devoid of aesthetic or any other redeeming value now strikes a chord in my greedy angling heart. I mean, I know I'll be back there. I hope with a good friend like John to share the experience with. Damselflies and a few good trout managed to pound a pretty good number on my brain.

Beartooth
Mountains

*A*ll kinds of wild things happen all at once. A manic electrical storm rides over the granite crest over there. The wind turns frigid and swirls in cyclonic gusts. And a large female golden trout attacks a Muddler Minnow bouncing across the smoky green streambed.

The fish flashes crimson, slashing at the streamer while planing sideways in the current.

Lightning sizzles, closer now, among mountains that look like the busted teeth of a punched-out Rush Street wino. Ragged suckers with patches of dirty melting snow holding out in shadowed nooks against the heat of a brief alpine summer.

These are the Beartooths of south-central Montana, about fifty miles southwest of Billings by air. Hundreds of lakes are here, both named and unnamed. Some lie above ten thousand feet and entail a brutal hike, often with long stretches of straight-up scrambling and climbing and sweating. Thoughts run to Why in the hell am I here doing this crazy bullshit anyway? No one in their right mind goes backpacking of their own free will, or a variation on this time-worn, frustrated theme.

Mentioning a choice piece of water is not often wise, particularly if it holds sizable goldens, but if you can make it to this one you've earned the right to fish for these guys. The stroll there is a lung-burning, all-too-often bushwhacking killer. It is called Lightning Lake and it is a bitch to get to, even with the earnest directions of someone from the local department of fish and game office. Lying well over 9,000 feet, Lightning is about sixty acres with a maximum depth of 122 feet. Goldens over ten pounds have been surveyed here by members of the department, but they are almost impossible to catch unless you find them on the feed or in the connecting streams on the spawning move. Then they can be taken—sometimes. Right after ice-out, normally in mid to late July, is the best time to make a trip of at least three nights here. You'll need the stay to recuperate from the "walk" in, and you'll want a healthy chunk of time to chase the goldens.

The golden I am racing the storm with right now is played quickly, brought to shore, and admired for its riotous color scheme that features reds, emeralds, oranges, blacks, and whites. I return the trout to the stream and the creature streaks across the current, disappearing under moss-covered rocks.

It has taken us a while to figure out that the way to entice the goldens into striking is by using a streamer with some flash and pop to it, like the Muddlers or a Zonker or a Flashabou Woolly Bugger. Things like these turn the trick. A 6-weight with a seven-and-a-half-foot leader tapered to 4X is ideal for this work. The streamer is cast to the head of the pool, allowed to sink to the stream's bottom, and then stripped in jerks right in front of and past the grouped males and females. Sometimes a dozen or more casts are required, but when the strike comes—and it always does, eventually—it is fierce, savage, territorial. The fish do not brook intrusions while they are high under the influence of the procreation dance.

When working the lakes with streamers, casting well ahead of cruising trout and stripping in the fly seems to produce. Prospecting the water with sinking tips and streamers also helps find the fish. There are also rare times of abundance when the water boils with rising goldens. When this happens, pattern selection is of little importance. Any dry cast upon the surface that approximates the naturals will take fish. But don't count on this happening in your lifetime. I've only seen this occur once, despite my numerous trips to golden waters.

The heavy weather is close to me, the air charged. I throw the rod aside and walk away from it. Being drilled by a lightning bolt

seems a very distinct possibility. Shelter is called for. A place to
hide. The lee side of a large boulder turns the natural trick. Rain,
hail, thunder, and white light pound across the sky above me.
It's midafternoon but the day is dark for a while there. Then the
storm is gone. Remnants of its nastiness swirl around steel gray
summits in the south.

The air has cooled. Scents from the moistened grasses, wildflowers, and mosses mix in pleasant combinations. The sun comes
out and burns the rain off the rocks. This happens fast. You can
see the water shrink quickly by evaporation.

The next fish fights hard, and I run after a pink-and-orange
golden of several pounds as it zips down out of a turquoise run
through water that is not deep enough to cover its back. Through
two more pools, then the trout soars over a miniature waterfall,
crashing in the water. Spray from the concussion shoots out and
away in an undisciplined circle. The fish is tiring but still struggles,
using its wide girth for resistance in the current. The golden can
be moved slowly toward me with force from the rod. The conflict,
having burst suddenly into life, stops abruptly when the trout turns
on its side and quits the game.

What a fantastic fish. In crystal light the golden shimmers a
natural riot of color way out here above timberline. In my most
optimistic fly-fishing fantasies I could not have imagined a trip
better than this one. To get to these special lakes requires a hike
of many miles that courses up and over several high rocky divides
before winding severely upward into the remote terrain.

This is high, barren land where only specialized plants can survive the harsh climate. Even in late July large fields of snow
remain, and wildflowers cover the ground in a celebration of the
nearly simultaneous arrival of spring and summer then, shortly,
fall. The mountains are all around us as my party works its way
across a level basin to a series of lakes connected by a narrow
cascading band of water.

There must be over a thousand lakes in this wilderness with
fish, and some of them have goldens. Most of the best lakes are
above nine thousand feet, and the fish grow large, over five pounds.

A nice golden taken in the Beartooths.

We see trout of these dimensions lying motionless in the water like suspended bars of heavy metal. Just down below this thin trail traversing a cliff above a lake is where we will fish.

Our timing is right, and we hit the fish as they are moving out of the lakes and into the streams at the beginning of spawning. The goldens are full of energy, muscular, and they glow with breeding intensity. Bunches of them wriggle across water running shallow over the rocks as we cross the stream. They are everywhere now, moving always upstream.

Goldens are legendary for being capricious, difficult-to-catch trout. You can hike in and up, always up, for miles to "world-class" locations, only to discover that the fish are not feeding. Nothing will change this situation except the trout. But now that they are in moving water the fishing is simplified somewhat. Even in their agitated state, they will often ignore the streamer, even though it sometimes bumps one right in the snout. The fish have more important things to concentrate on right now.

Often the trout will bat the pattern away with their noses, hitting the hook as if with a tennis backhand, but eventually they do strike. The goldens are powerful but not acrobatic, preferring to charge to the bottom of the stream and hold tight against the line. As they tire, pressure from the angler brings them to the surface, where they thrash the water and shoot back and forth in shorter and shorter runs. The battles last mere minutes but seem much longer. Finding a quiet piece of water to land and release the golden often takes more time than the actual playing of the fish.

In their native waters of the Kern River drainage in California's Sierra Mountains (and in a lake near my home in northwest Montana) a golden of twelve inches is a trophy, a fish to be admired and cherished. But in these waters, along with those of the Big Horns and the Wind Rivers of Wyoming down south a little bit, fish of two and three pounds are not rare. A friend of mine has taken the species to seven pounds. The world record is around eleven, and fisheries biologists have tagged specimens over a dozen pounds, a size impossible for me to visualize.

The cartoonlike coloration possibly evolved as protection against ultraviolet radiation that rains down on the fish in heavy dosages at high altitude. Or maybe it is a means of blending in with the gravels of their native streams, a way to protect against predation from above.

I do not know or care too much right now. These are minor details in a surreal festival of piscatorial proportions. Even the little lake resting down below camp is filled with the fish, though in smaller sizes. Casting drys at the inlets and outlets and along the shore near rock piles and outcroppings produces plenty of trout running up to fourteen inches, strong fighters with all the color of their bigger relations above. A trip to catch only these goldens would have been far more than satisfying.

The all-too-brief stay settles into a daily pattern of breakfast, checking leaders, selecting patterns, several hours of chasing trout and enjoying the isolation, a quick romp back to shelter, usually with static electricity crackling through the air, an hour or two of lounging around camp, dinner, and then late-night conversation around a fire or under a sizable tarp if the rains come after sunset.

Except for the fabric roof above us, we are exposed to the blasts of weather that are a daily feature here. The thunder reverberates through the surrounding rock walls, shifting in tone and often intensifying as it funnels down hard-rock corridors. I can feel the blasts buffet the air, and the lightning raises cain with my night vision. Then, as swiftly as the storm appears it vanishes, and the Milky Way takes its place, a bright, solid-looking band stretching across a now discernibly purple sky. Meteors fizzle about, sputtering all over the place. Sleep, then dawn seems to show up only minutes later. The good, free life in feral splendor.

The last golden I catch is the best of the trip for me. The others in the party are casting nymphs, drys, and streamers from rocky points out into the lake at the stream's outlet — with little success. The few trout that are rising display extremely selective habits. Upstream a brief distance is a long narrow piece of water that looks like a combination glide-pool-riffle. Lush grass and moss grow down to the edge of the flow. Tiny pink flowers blanket the green. The water slides darkly through here, but a pod of goldens, holding in the current, is visible about twenty feet ahead.

For the sake of variety I cast a Spruce Fly well ahead of the fish, watching it sink and tumble back toward me. As soon as the streamer hits bottom I strip in the line, causing the imitation to slide across the leading edge of trout. From somewhere hidden under the bank a bright yellow torpedo rockets out and crunches the fly, then does an about-face and races back to cover. Feeling the bite of the hook, the golden flashes up to the head of the pool, flailing crazily in an attempt to navigate a cascade of several feet.

The fish almost makes the top and the pool above, but the rushing water is too much and it's spent after three tries. I hold the fish in my hands: over twenty inches long and almost half a foot deep, with a pronounced kype and only a few black spots on its tail. An electric rainbow of a fish of maybe four pounds. I want to hold this one forever, to enjoy its color and size. It is the reason for my being here, and the trip is complete now. No need to take any more of these trout. They would all be beautiful but after the fact. Anticlimaxes.

"Put it back, John," a voice says in my head. I listen to these things on occasion, so I revive the big guy in the icy calm of an eddy near shore. In an instant the golden surges from my hands and is gone like a well-executed illusion. And I wonder . . .

Had the golden ever been here in the first place?

Grayling
Lakes

W_{ay} back in the mountains where the snow and ice hang around
sometimes until mid-August, there are a few lakes that still hold
a special prize—grayling.

These are beautiful fish with gun-metal gray bodies punctuated
with black spots and yellow-and-white slashes of color on their fins.

When the family hound was younger, he and I used to chase
them frequently, briefly escaping the noisome distractions even
a small town like Whitefish creates. You know, the usual things:
exotic driving habits, the Lycra-clad bike crew, moose in the Safe-
way parking lot. Tough stuff.

Grayling are unique among their salmonid brethren because of
their large dorsal fins—saillike appendages flecked with bright
drops of turquoise. The dog has jumped overboard from our canoe
when the fish were around in large numbers, dimpling the surface
of some off-the-wall lake hidden among the pines and often surrounded by malarial bogs. As with squirrels, this dog has never
come close to a grayling.

A fifty-pound dog leaping out of a canoe with dedicated enthusiasm is an interesting experience in a wet sort of way. Trying
to maintain balance as this commotion explodes like grouse from
cover is difficult, and tipping over is not unheard of. I've never
lost any gear or anything, and the sight of the dog swimming madly
to and fro snapping at widening riseforms is a pleasant form of
entertainment, even when viewed from water level. I've wondered
what the fish think (surely some form of primitive thought must

91

occur) as this large, white, very furry animal paddles back and forth, disrupting their feeding activity.

To watch these fish rise to midges that approach microscopic dimensions in the clear water of a mountain lake, the prominent dorsal breaking the water, sharklike, as it chases down the diminutive prey, is a moment always frozen in time, much like the lakes themselves during a dead-cold January.

My fascination, briefly turned obsession, with grayling began when I was eleven and still too young to see an addiction when the sucker looked me straight in the eyes. While spending a weekend with my grandparents, I watched several old black-and-white 16-mm movies taken on a long-ago trip to the Northwest Territories in Canada. My grandparents were young when the movies were taken and they traveled everywhere seeking trout, salmon, and, in general, an angling good time.

They were casting drys into riffles in a small river densely lined with tag alder in one of these old films. Snow-covered peaks dominated a flickering background. Even with the poor film quality, the many fins waving back and forth above the water were unmistakable.

The two were fishing about fifty yards apart, and as the camera shifted its attention from one to the other, fish were constantly played and released. They were practicing catch and release way back then, or maybe they'd already taken enough for lunch. I prefer to believe the former. A close-up revealed a creature in my grandmother's hands that did not resemble any trout I had ever caught in my childishly brief fly-fishing career. Her fingers splayed the dorsal backward, fanlike—large, spotted, almost alien.

I watched the films several more times and from that night on was hooked, though the opportunity to cast over these curious fish did not come until twenty years later, on a lake in northwest Montana.

By then I was gainfully (barely) employed as a sports editor for a small-town daily paper in the region. Little money and some free time were the work's chief assets. The spare hours I devoted to searching for grayling. The quest was eventually consummated

This grayling hit a small dry.

at a little lake lying among larch and lodgepole in the low mountains west of town.

Word of the magic water came from an ad salesman at the paper. So, armed with directions, a sixteen-foot canoe, and great expectations, the dog and I struck out for the lake early one day-off morning.

Getting there involved a two-hour drive, always up, past small bright streams and dark beaver ponds. In one of these a moose was standing shoulder-deep in the water chomping on aquatic plants.

The sight of this animal drove the dog nuts and he pawed his way across my lap and out the window, hitting the road at about twenty miles an hour, landing with the grace of an empty paint can being bounced from the back of a truck. Sorting himself out, he swiftly gave chase, but by then the moose was gracefully (surprisingly so considering the animal's ungainly shape) disappearing into the pines of a nearby ridge.

This incident was not without ramifications for the pickup and myself, because we clattered off the road and into a small gully, severely upsetting the cassette-tape deck, which kicked into over-drive, blasting Steely Dan's "Aja" at 78-rpm speed. A quick inspection over an ice-cold beer plucked from the upended styrofoam cooler showed that no body or structural damage had occurred. The dog returned, wet and dirty, and we were soon off again.

A few more miles of dusty driving through forest, then stark clear-cut, then forest—an ugly, unending pattern—took us to a lake of emerald water with a shore of moss-covered deadfalls and steep drop-offs. Grayling were rising all over the place, splashing, slurping, and smacking the surface with the enthusiasm of early summer, a season when winter no longer seems real or possible.

I cast flies for hours amid the wired feeding with no success. The famed dorsals charged the canoe, turquoise spots wild with fluorescent energy. Patterns ranging from a #14 Adams to a #2 Marabou Muddler were blasted frantically through the air with artful futility. The dog threatened to dive overboard, but I strongly suggested otherwise. He eventually fell asleep in the front of the canoe.

Back on shore during lunch, the woods vibrating with the hum of billions of tiny insects, I considered the problem.

Then a large fish started working right in front of us, next to a partially submerged log. Leaving the dog asleep on top of a dead-fall, I crept to the bank and watched as a grayling sucked in the smallest insects imaginable.

Fly boxes were flung open with abandon, their contents rifled, but the best offerings I uncovered were only #22s, and the little buggers on the water looked to be #26 at the largest.

Concentrating on the fish working by me, I cast just ahead of the anticipated feeding direction, and on the third attempt a hungry grayling rocketed up from the bottom and hammered the fly. The pressure of the line sent the fish in a frenetic, circling dash to deeper water. On a six-foot rod with a fine tippet, this was good sport. After several minutes the grayling reluctantly came to shore. Whether from fear or anger, its colors were intense: Day-Glow yellows. Perfect whites. The silver now shining with a purple tint. And the turquoise on that special fin. The blue would have shamed a robin's egg.

After admiring the fish, I turned it loose.

I caught and released countless grayling as the sun worked past the western tree line. The fish ranged from one to two pounds, and all displayed the intense coloration I'd observed in the first one.

Later on I managed to take fish on #16 caddis and mayfly imitations, and even on Woolly Worms, but the tiny dry flies always proved the most consistent producers, especially on 6X or 7X tippet.

From that day on, grayling were definitely a big part of my angling madness.

Normally a fish of moving water, grayling are most often found in lakes in Montana. There are only a few grayling left in their original riverine habitats—maybe three thousand in the Big Hole and perhaps one thousand in the Madison. These are threatened by proposed logging but are hanging on for the present.

Grayling have been around this part of the planet longer than most other salmonids. Their original waters extended right to the faces of the massive glaciers that marked the last ice age. The fish evolved into creatures that could tolerate, even thrive, in the harsh cold. Cold clear water is now their specialty.

I eventually took grayling in rivers, small streams, and other lakes, but the search was often higher, where the trees thinned and grew stunted and snarled from the wind and short growing season.

Just across the North Fork of the Flathead River, close to the western mountain wall of the Livingston Range in Glacier National Park, lies the lower but rugged Whitefish Range. This is an area of dense fir, larch, and lodgepole. Small streams and high mountain lakes are relatively untouched by anglers and others. This is home to grizzlies, gray wolves, bald eagles, and possibly the mountain caribou.

Grayling are found here, also.

A typical northwest Montana grayling lake.

The water is clean, undisturbed, and deep in one lake I fish, an important consideration in an area where snowfall often approaches one thousand inches and ice depths are measured in feet. The lake is rarely accessible before mid-June, and usually later. A good deal of map-reading and conversation with other fly fishers turned up its location.

Before the snow melts and the logging road opens for casual traffic, you must hike in. Not far, maybe a couple of miles after a rough, steeply climbing drive. With a light daypack the walk burns the lungs a little, but the warmth of late-spring sunshine, the sound of running water, the smell of pine, and the sound of marmots whistling among the rocks is suitable compensation. Rounding a turn in the trail, an avalanche chute choked with tons of snow, ice, and mangled trees is visible, its leading edge extending well out into the blue water. The western shore is the first to open. Grayling will be spotted working among the boulders and shelves. In the east the peaks of Glacier scream into the sky. A thick blanket of deep green forest fills in the valley. The lake is twenty acres of perfection filled with small, playful grayling that rise every time I come here.

A very special place.

Rigging a travel rod always takes longer than it should. The sounds of the fish make me nervous and my fingers clumsy. Finally a minuscule bit of feathered brown nonsense is attached to a spider-silk-diameter leader. The first casts are sent out over the surface, the water so smooth that the line's reflection on it is a mirror image of the reality flying above.

With some luck the fly falls in step with a feeding grayling, and the take comes as the fish shoots through the water column. Silver brilliance surging toward the light, and then the fish drops down with the tiny pattern stuck in its tough-skinned mouth. The grayling of this lofty lake fight well, frequently sounding with a determination that sends a discernible vibration back along the line. Eventually the fish gives up and I drag it to shore, maybe ten inches with those turquoise spots on the dorsal fin.

Unhooking the grayling as it lies on its side is an unsettling experience. Its eye bores through me as I remove the fly. As if the fish is saying "I know why you need to be here, but you're only a visitor. This is our turf." Or something to that effect. Alpine madness is a benign affliction.

And this sensation is a touch spooky, but reassuring all the same.

To know that the species is being reintroduced in Michigan, thriving with characteristic grayling flair in Canada and Alaska, and hanging on in Montana is encouraging.

As the day progresses and the desire to keep casting wanes, there is a favorite rock outcropping that affords an expansive view of the action. There always seem to be eagles soaring overhead, marmots talking among the scree, and sometimes there are fresh tracks from a grizzly that foraged recently on freshly green plant shoots in the south-facing avalanche chutes nearby.

The sun is gone now behind the peaks, and the lake's surface is dark. Time for the hike back to the truck. A quick look back at the water and the feeding grayling. Their riseforms are everywhere.

Do they ever stop?

Hidden
Lake

*L*ofty visions filled with waves of jagged mountain peaks, driving the vertiginous Going-to-the-Sun Road, and silver-tipped grizzly bears all come to mind when I think of Glacier National Park.

And with good reason. Glacier is one of the most unique and spectacular playgrounds on the planet. It sits in my backyard, less than thirty minutes from home just off on the eastern horizon. I can see some of its peaks from my driveway. Where Yellowstone is a park, Glacier reminds me more of a wilderness, and I'll take the wild side of things every time.

Yet there is another facet to Glacier that is often overlooked by most visitors. Quality fishing.

While the park's kindred sister, Yellowstone, is justly famous for its world-class trout waters, Glacier receives little if any attention from serious or neophyte anglers.

Which is too bad, because within the park's boundaries are some quality lakes and streams. Not in Yellowstone's class, to be sure. But, on the other hand, they are not choked with people flinging an assortment of flies and hardware in standing-room-only fashion.

I first discovered the angling in Glacier during the early 1970s when I hiked in to Hidden Lake from a trail at Logan Pass. The scenery was its usual grand self, the goats were their usual nonchalant selves, and Hidden Lake shone in clear, turquoise splendor. But there was more. Much more for a fishing devotee like me.

Two individuals were working the barren shoreline, casting small dry flies to cruising cutthroat trout. More often than not the trout would either flee for cover as soon as the pattern hit the lake's surface, or nose up to the fly and then turn disdainfully away in search of a more appropriate food source. There were a number of these fish in the one- and two-pound class, and every now and then one would succumb to temptation and hit a dry fly. The fish were deep-bodied and strong, putting up a good fight before they were netted and released.

After a while curiosity overcame angling etiquette and I approached the two men to ask about the park's fishing. They were kind and helpful and the following hour's conversation opened up a fascinating fishing world for me. High mountain lakes surrounded by glacial cirques and rarely touched by man, wild rivers and streams full of grayling, cutthroat, brookies, and rainbows, all set in one of the most beautiful locations in the world. Beautiful and usually tough to reach or, for that matter, find.

In the ensuing years I've spent many hours probing Glacier's watery secrets. I've been shut out often to be sure. That's the nature of high-mountain fishing. But I've never been disappointed. The chance to escape the crowds and fish for wild trout is a reward in itself.

And there have been those magic times when the fish abandoned all sense of propriety and hammered any fly or lure tossed in their vicinity.

There are a variety of gamefish in the park. Among them are brook trout, westslope cutthroat trout, Yellowstone cutthroat trout, hybrids of these two species and/or rainbows, bull trout, grayling, kokanee salmon, lake trout, rainbows, whitefish, and northern pike.

The park's waters eventually drain into three large bodies of water—the Pacific Ocean, the Gulf of Mexico, and Hudson Bay. Each drainage varies noticeably from the other. The Pacific waters include the North and Middle forks of the Flathead River, which all merge into the Flathead River and on to the Clark Fork and finally into the Columbia River. The area has dense stands of conifers, along with narrow, ice-scoured valleys that often contain large lakes. The streams are usually small, fed by snowmelt, and are relatively infertile due to a lack of nutrients.

Bowman, Kintla, and McDonald lakes can all be reached by road and are best fished in the late spring and early summer from a canoe or float tube. Occasionally, especially after ice-out in early summer, the cutthroats will move into the shallows to feed on emerging insects and minnows. At times like these a small caddis or even an Adams at the end of a long, slender leader (6X) will take fish. The scenery is mind-blowing, deer are browsing all over the place, and grizzlies are often lurking in the woods. I love the great bears. Wyoming's Wind Rivers are wonderful country, but without the grizzly, the experience takes on pleasant but sedate, calmer overtones. The juice that comes from sighting a big bear working a hillside while you are casting cannot be matched. No petting zoos here. No "Keep off the grass" signs. No bullshit. There's nothing better.

These lakes are all beautiful, with towering mountains casting their reflections on the pristine waters. Lake McDonald is just to the north of the lower reaches of the Going-to-the-Sun Road, so there is food, lodging, and other amenities available at Apgar and McDonald Lodge. The lake itself is lousy fishing: The water is too sterile. Both the Middle and North forks of the Flathead River are largely migration corridors for cutthroat and bull trout that move up from Flathead Lake in late spring and early summer, often traveling well over a hundred miles to reach their spawning beds in small feeder creeks. There are few resident trout, and they are mostly on the small side. In other words, marginal fishing most of the time.

Roads along the North Fork are an intriguing proposition, because they run through some dense forest, mainly lodgepole. Both the east-side road in the park and the west-side road are gravel-and-dirt affairs that require the complete attention of any driver. Logging trucks, deer, and downed trees are a frequent hazard.

Don't expect restaurants and motels up this way. There are primitive (read "outhouses") campgrounds at Logging Creek, Quartz Creek, Bowman Creek and Lake, and at the North Fork, along with one at Kintla Lake. There are only two "towns" along the river — Polebridge and Moose City. Polebridge is little more than a general store, some homes, a youth hostel (I recently was forced to stay in one while fishing in Iceland when my hotel arrangements disintegrated. I'm too far gone to appreciate the communal experience. I don't like youth hostels.), and the distinctive Northern Lights Saloon that is only occasionally open. There are no phone or electric power lines here, either. Moose City is the location of the U.S. and Canadian customs stations, some homes, and another store. The U.S. item looks like an Aspen condo—a lot of money spent to guard a dirt-road border in the middle of nowhere. From the crossing on north the road remains primitive, winding through forest, clear-cuts (always clear-cuts), and some cabins.

Winters here are long and brutal, but with the warm weather comes the sound of rushing water everywhere. Wildflowers explode into bloom and all is right with the world. Trails, many of them death marches, reach most of the major streams and lakes in both Glacier's Livingston Range and the Whitefish Range to the west in the Flathead National Forest. Rustic campsites are at almost every turn of the path.

Although all of the streams have some resident cutthroat and bull trout, the best fishing during summer's peak is in the high mountain lakes.

Avalanche Lake, just off Going-to-the-Sun, is a comparatively easy two-mile hike. Waterfalls pour down from the surrounding cliffs. The best fishing is another mile's hike to the head of the lake, for cutthroat trout. Lincoln Lake lies at the bottom of thirteen-hundred-foot Beaver Chief Falls, has decent fishing for cutthroat, and offers plenty of solitude because the eight-mile trail dead-ends at the lake.

Most of the region east of the Continental Divide is much drier than the west. The high peaks knock much of the moisture out of any weather system before it makes it over to the plains. The waters that drain toward the Gulf of Mexico are no exception. The forests contain stunted stands of wind-battered pines and aspen.

Grizzlies frequently come down out of the glacial valleys and roam the plains in search of a local rancher's sheep or one of the many honeybee hives. The bears are usually shot or maybe captured and relocated on the Blackfeet Reservation, much to the joy of tribal members. Just what they need, a thundering horde of problem grizzlies.

Glacier's best fishing is in the lakes, which are a bit more fertile, meaning they support adequate (barely) populations of aquatic insect life to sustain fishable trout numbers. The rivers and creeks here hold small populations of mostly small fish that are hardly worth the angler's time and effort.

Gunsight Lake offers challenging fishing for chunky rainbows that, with their silver sides, resemble steelhead. This is a difficult hike of six miles to a relatively comfortable campground. The fly fisherman will frequently run into great dry-fly action during the summer evenings when a variety of hatches dance their way through the season. Another nice hike is the eleven-mile round trip from the Cut Bank Ranger Station to Medicine Grizzly Lake, which is full of foot-long, skinny rainbows.

Brook trout aficionados should take the tour boat from the head of Two Medicine Lake for a two-mile hike to Upper Two Medicine Lake, work their way up the north shore to the inlet, and then fish all the way back for fat brook trout. Brook trout are brook trout wherever they are found, and Glacier's are no exception. They are not very difficult to catch.

Sherburne Lake has the distinction of being the ugliest lake in Glacier because of heavy irrigation drawdown that exposes its gooey mud banks. It does contain a number of large northerns for anyone who wants to fish over them.

The Hudson Bay drainage is dominated by the Belly and Waterton rivers. The country offers quality backpacking in relative solitude, along with some top-notch brook trout, grayling, and rainbow fishing. Elizabeth Lake is reached from both Chief Mountain Customs and from Many Glacier through the Ptarmigan Tunnel. This is a spectacular but lung-expanding trip that offers high-altitude vistas of magnificent proportions. Elizabeth is excellent fishing for grayling and rainbow. There are a number of small, marshy, mosquito-infested lakes in this area that also contain large brook trout that are rarely fished for because of their remoteness and the frequent closings due to grizzlies. A conversation with a park ranger concerning location and current status is advisable.

Waterton River flows into Waterton Lake (astoundingly), which lies in both Glacier and Waterton Lakes National Park in Canada. It offers marginal fishing for whitefish.

For the fly fisherman, an eight-foot six-inch, 6-weight travel rod with a weight-forward and medium sinking-tip line is the best bet. A fly selection that includes Royal Wulffs, Adamses, Elk Hair Caddises, hopper patterns, and Goddard Caddises in sizes #14 to #18 will work well. A few Muddler Minnows and Woolly Worms (olive is best) from #6 to #10 will cover a few more bases. Add several nymphs in shades of gray and brown, such as a Hare's Ear, around #12 to #16, and most situations can be handled.

About the bears. They rarely bother anyone if they are left alone. Make noise when hiking or fishing, especially in areas of rushing water, which drown out many sounds. When camping, store food well away from sleeping areas and don't cook near tents or sleeping bags. (The park gives each visitor a pamphlet that goes into specifics on this subject.)

Summer squalls whipping through the mountains can drop the temperature more than twenty degrees in less than an hour. A day that promises temperatures in the eighties can end up cold, wet, and in the forties with hypothermia a very real possibility.

All of this sounds pretty casual. "Sure. There's great fishing just a few miles up the trail" type stuff, but hiking in the park is not easy. Much of the travel is on straight-up switchback terrain. And for those of us with world-class cases of acrophobia, certain trails should be avoided, unless crawling on your belly like a reptile is your idea of fun. Some of the trails are long and demand that an individual be in good shape. A good insect repellent is also a necessity. Glacier grows some quality mosquitoes and other biting flying creatures.

The last time I fished Glacier was one of the best times. Late September, cool, high clouds, and patches of sunlight shooting through onto the tundra up above Logan Pass as my sister Anne and I hiked the three miles up and down on our way to Hidden Lake and its wary population of Yellowstone cutthroats. I had not fished there in a few years and was eager to see how the trout were doing. From a vantage point hundreds of feet above the water we could see the riseforms of feeding fish. Several late-season tourists were soaking in the view from the wooden overlook behind us. We headed down, tracking back and forth on the uneven, rocky trail. My knees were rubber by the time we reached bottom, and looking up I thought God, the climb back looks like a hell of a good time.

We stopped and munched some chips and salsa while sitting on a boulder that jutted out into the lake. There were not any fish rising now where we were, so I headed down along the lake's shore, hoping to spot working cutts. Mountain peaks jutted far above. The undergrowth was shifting from green to rust, gold, yellow, purple, and orange. There was no breeze. Everything was silent. Where the path neared the lake I stopped and scanned the water for fish. After several minutes I spotted a trout cruising not far from shore—large, solid-looking, yellow-orange metallic.

I hurried back and retrieved Anne and my gear. Rigging up, I cast a Hare's Ear well ahead of the next working fish and let the nymph sink a couple of feet to the trout's level. A slight twitch and the fish opened its jaws wide, the white of its mouth clearly visible through the clear water. The trout charged the fly from twenty feet. I had to make a conscious effort to avoid striking too soon. The cutthroat thrashed and then came to shore quickly —not much of a fight. It looked a good deal like a large golden with few spots but hues on its flanks shading from gold to orange. The spots near the tail, thinly along the back, and up through the shoulders were large and very black. Eighteen inches of poor-fighting, exotically pretty trout.

The fish slipped the hook while I admired it from above on my rocky perch. I quickly stripped line and cast out to another, larger trout. Line whizzed above, unerringly snagging in a fir tree behind me. I broke off the nymph, tied on another, and immediately snagged it. Then another and another, and my sister seemed

Hidden Lake harbors Yellowstone cutthroat. This shot was taken in late September.

to think this was quite humorous in her own quiet way. Taking
time to settle down, I tied on an Atlantic salmon fly I had in one
box—a Blue Charm (I carry all sorts of marginally useless patterns
with me, not unlike every other fly fisher I know).

The thing was heavy, landing with a splash and sinking quickly.
Despite the disturbance, a trout saw the pattern and smashed it
with determination. Very selective fish here today—typical mountain-lake fly fishing. When the trout are feeding, everything
works—when they're off the bite, nothing takes fish. A crapshoot
in a rarefied atmosphere. Another brief thrash and a meek ride
to shore. This one was perhaps twenty inches and colored like
its smaller cousin. These were attractive fish that were fun to catch
but could not or would not fight worth a damn. Maybe the water
was too cold: It felt like ice on my hands. Maybe the season was
too far gone and they had winter on their minds. Who knows.
I didn't care.

We caught a few more, then struck out back uphill. The hike
was strenuous and we stopped to catch our breath and sip water
a bunch of times along the way. Near the top of our climb we
paused and looked back at Hidden. The trout were again visibly
rising.

Knowing this was my last time here this year was a sweet feeling
in a lonely, satisfying kind of way—a distant, almost "from another world" sensation that is special to fishing and to the high
country of Glacier.

This unnamed emotion is the reason I come here in the first
place.

Mission
Mountains

Watching wild cutthroat trout dimple the surface of a wilderness lake is an appropriate way to say good-bye to the high country for another year, especially if you have just come down from a lake even farther up the drainage that holds a marginal population of small, brightly colored golden trout.

October in the Mission Mountains. Clear skies. Special light. Warm days. Ice-cold nights filled with a billion stars. And trout feeding with an intent seen only in autumn. Winter is coming. Make the most of what little time remains before snow and ice lock up the country.

The Missions hold a firm place in my heart. They have for years. Even with the hordes of Boy Scouts, weekend backpackers, and day-hiking granolas, the mountains remain a place of escape and solitude. Trails run along tiny streams that tumble down from out of rarely visited lakes backed up against impassive glacial cirques. These paths head off from secret locations hidden from the view of those driving dusty logging roads. A couple of hours of steep hiking through dense pine forest, up, over and under dead-falls, through swampy meadows, and across ankle-threatening scree slopes reveals clusters of pure lakes often full of westslope cutthroat trout or maybe rainbows or brookies from plantings in the 1930s. Knife-edged ridges and jagged peaks block the view to the west. Fields of snow and tiny pockets of ice, remnants of the last ice age, cover the rock. The snow and blue ice is tinted with the pink and gray dust of wind-blasted rock. Campsites are

A lake high on the eastern flank of the Mission Mountains.

where you find them. Level ground is in short supply. So is wood
for a fire. I carry enough in my pack for a small fire on the last
night. But water, the best-tasting anywhere, runs, jumps, and cas-
cades from cliffs, holes in the ice, and outlets of these lakes.

There is one region the dog and I go to each fall. It is our way
of taking in the loneliness and power of country unspoiled by
logging and development. A way of fixing untamed visions that
will carry us through a long winter and into the joy and freedom
of a new spring. Taking the trout on drys is a part of this, too.
So is keeping two small cutthroats for a last supper of sorts. The
fish always taste of the Missions — of the pine and cold water and
granite. Only butter in a hot pan — that is all they need. Then a
little bourbon mixed with lake water and a cigar smoked while
standing with my head thrown back soaking in the sky, a hemi-
sphere of bright lights that has dropped down through the thin
air up here to surround me. The dog is off sniffing for marmots
in a rockfall across the lake. We are alone, and the awareness that

I could disappear without a trace or touch of guilt concerning familial responsibility is both reassuring and frightening.

Fly fishing in the Missions is classic high-country trout action. When the fish are feeding, any dry will take them: Wulff, Adams, Humpy, caddis. What is used does not matter; any cast that hits the water without too much disturbance will turn a trout. On days when warm air rises up the mountains in a rush of puffy wind, grasshoppers, ants, and beetles fool the fish who have keyed in to the unexpected meal delivered from the valley below. Fishing hoppers at seventy-five hundred feet seems a bit strange at first, but the cutthroat do not seem to mind.

Then there are the times of angling famine when nothing seems to work. A lake that boiled with rising trout the night before can seem lifeless and devoid of fish the next day. At times like these, dry flies rarely produce. About the only thing I hope for is to spot cruising trout and then cautiously drop an olive Woolly Worm (with a tuft of crimson for a tail) well in front of a fish, then wait for the perfect moment to twitch the thing. Often this terrifies the cutthroat, and it flees. Occasionally the little blip of life triggers a rush and a take. Fifty-fifty is a good percentage of success under these conditions. Blind-casting a nymph like a Hare's Ear with a sinking tip is slow, boring work, but persistence will usually yield a trout or two, often the largest in the lake.

That is in essence mountain-lake fishing. Simplified of course, but pretty much the state of the pursuit. A 5-weight rod with floating and Sink-Tip lines, some Woolly Worms, Adamses, caddis, and a few nymphs pretty well covers the possibilities. Add a few hoppers and Muddlers, and that is about it. Minnows are not likely inhabitants of alpine waters, so most streamers take fish as a result of trout curiosity, and possibly territorial tendencies.

As I said earlier, I love the Missions, but driving along the Swan Valley is no longer a pleasant experience. Looking west toward the wilderness, massive clear-cuts run right up to and sometimes illegally into the Missions. Greed and an insane disrespect for nature are responsible for gradual destruction of the area.

Driving along the dirt-and-rock roads of the Jim Creek drainage of the Swan River in this part of northwest Montana is gut-wrenching, ugly stuff these days, and not just because of the many bumps, potholes, and ruts.

What was once a beautiful northern Rockies forest that flowed wonderfully silent and green up to the sharp peaks, sheer cliffs, and blue-white snowfields of the Missions is now acre upon acre of brutal clear-cut, all made since the late eighties. The once clean waters of the drainage, including the West Fork of Jim Creek, are now often clouded with silt, and the colorful streambed gravels are choking in the stuff that comes tumbling down from the logging roads and scarred land with the spring runoff and each rain.

Clear-cutting and road-building in the area by Plum Creek Timber Company has led to a die-off of native bull trout. Plum Creek, Burlington Northern's timber operation here in the Northwest, is in the process of cutting all of its merchantable timber in a cut-and-run program fueled by fear of a possible leveraged buyout and good old corporate avarice.

"This is not a sustained yield program," said Bill Parson, director of Plum Creek operations for the Rocky Mountain Region during a press tour in the region in the fall of 1989. "We are not on a sustained yield program. We have never said we were on a sustained yield program, and we have never been on a sustained yield program. Let's get to the heart of it: Sure it's extensively logged, but what is wrong with that?"

The bull trout is one of the largest freshwater salmonids in the world and is closely related to the lake and brook trouts. It occasionally exceeds twenty pounds, and the average weight of those caught in northwest Montana is around eight pounds. When these fish make their spawning run out of Flathead Lake up the Middle and North forks of the Flathead River, they may swim as much as 150 miles to reach their home waters in British Columbia.

Unfortunately, in this part of Montana, which holds some of the continent's finest bull trout water, every major spawning tributary is threatened by logging, according to a 1987 study endorsed by the American Fisheries Society. Not just one or two creeks, but every single stream providing spawning gravels for these fish could be gone by the turn of the century. This includes most of the creeks pouring out of the western slopes of the Missions.

Bull trout tried to spawn in Jim Creek following the logging, but the emerging embryos suffocated and rotted in the strangling quarter-inch or smaller fine sediments of the ruined stream. A study by the Montana Department of Fish, Wildlife and Parks revealed nearly a one hundred percent mortality rate in embryos caused by sedimentation, which deprives eggs and embryos of life-giving oxygen. The study was prompted by complaints in 1988 from a local resident who noticed unusual turbidity in the portion of Jim Creek that flows by his property. Biologists believe that there has been a violation of Montana's water-quality laws at Jim Creek and brought this to the attention of the Montana Water Quality Bureau (a seven-thousand-dollar fine was eventually levied against Plum Creek for water-quality violations in a settlement that failed to recognize the findings of the MDFWP). The net effect on Plum Creek was a big zero. The company proceeded with preparations to clear-cut a similar drainage to the north a few miles. Who cares? To paraphrase Ronald Reagan, "if you've seen one tree, you've seen them all."

We're not talking fifty percent or even seventy-five percent, but nearly one hundred percent mortality in the drainage. An entire year's worth of bull trout, which are designated a species of special concern in this state, is lost. And the same fate awaits this year's spawning population. Trout eggs do not do very well in muck — not in Jim Creek and not in hundreds of other streams and rivers experiencing or about to experience a similar fate in the Northwest.

Bull trout only spawn in a half-dozen or so streams in the Swan River drainage, so their chances for survival in the future are tenuous at best. Logging in the drainage is being blamed by many in the area for the demise of what was once a quality fishery in the Swan River.

In an effort to draw attention to the devastation, the musicians Bob Weir of the Grateful Dead and John Oates of Hall and Oates, along with local, regional, and national environmental leaders

A nice cutthroat taken from a Mission Mountains lake.

mountain-biked over two hundred miles of logging roads in the Swan Valley in August 1990. Talking with Weir is an intense experience. His eyes bored right into my soul and there was no doubt that he was silently asking "Whose side are you on? What do you think about this devastation?" Our brief chat was interesting, to mildly understate the situation.

"They're monsters—heartless, soulless monsters and it's hard not to be smitten a little bit when you see a clear-cut," said Weir of the timber industry. "The loggers say that there are plenty of trees, that there will always be plenty of trees. Someone said that about the buffalo, too."

I'm glad there are individuals who devote their lives to fighting the rape of the Northwest, but I am not equipped to do the same. Too much staring into this ugly light would probably lead to severe depression and worse for me. I still need and find happiness in the backcountry of the Missions.

In my early twenties, before most of the logging occurred, I spent countless days hiking through these mountains. If there is a lake in this country that I have not fished, I'll be surprised. Wilderness like this often has ponds and spring-fed bogs that are not shown on any map, even the topos. Many times I've come into a clearing and discovered such a place. Despite ever-present swarms of mosquitoes, I always drop the pack and rig up the rod. I've caught cutthroats and brookies of twenty inches in little swampy holes no larger than a quarter-acre. All that seems to be needed is an inlet, outlet, and adequate depth to avoid freezing out. Slogging through muck above my knees, I've made off-balance casts to dead-looking water only to watch as a pack of marauding trout streaks from cover and attacks the fly. The first two fish are easy. After that, they grow wise and become wary. Three fish is a bonus. Four is a gift from the gods. For some reason, the cutthroats are always dark-colored with intense red slashes, and the brookies are the darkest green imaginable with blaze orange bellies and turquoise aureoles surrounding crimson spots. Electric trout hang out in these tiny pockets.

The air suddenly blows cool with a taste of snow. The cutthroats are still feeding along the shore. Clouds cover the sun. The dog brushes my legs and says in his own way that we should go now, back down to home. I get up from the log I am sitting on and shoulder my pack. Leaving is not easy. I can feel the pull to stay. A few yards down the trail I turn back for one last look. The mountaintops are covered in stormy weather. It is probably snowing on the goldens in the lake above.

The trout keep on feeding.

I'll be back next October. Count on it.

Ranch
Ponds

An hour or so south from Billings and just a little bit west of anywhere populated is some of the finest hunting for sharp-tailed grouse around. The birds are how I found the ranch-pond trout in the first place. Birds and trout. Trout and birds. The two are becoming constant companions. And now that I know a few other places to look for both east of the Divide, I manage to spend a good chunk of time flinging all sorts of strange patterns in prime waters and spraying assorted sizes of shot across far horizons, but that's moving ahead of the underappreciated game.

Looking out from a tall bluff in this wonderful open-ended country, I view the land I will work — going on for eternity and breaking off in a series of still-life waves first of pine forest, then of sage and small cactus and native grasses.

There is no breeze. No sound. The country stretches away silently, unreal, like a well-crafted relief map instead of tangible rock and earth.

The towering stacks of the power-generating plant a dozen miles distant at Colstrip flash a warning to the few aircraft that wander over in that direction.

Down in the ravines winding beneath parched piles of rock that have weathered the eons of wind, sun, and cold, you are startled from an ancient reverie by a dozen birds ripping into the clear light.

Shots are fired. Birds fall and you walk up the draw, jumping them once more. Two of our group have their limits of the grouse and it is time to move to the next twisted drainage to walk and dream and maybe shoot some more.

114

This is fantastic country, little hunted and full of grouse and pheasant and Hungarian partridge. Even some chukar and, as mentioned, lots of fat trout that could care less about their cousins laboring away in the hard-work turf found in the famous rivers and streams and creeks.

There is public land to hunt and several outfitters with leases to dozens of sections totaling hundreds of thousands of acres. And if the birds were not here in good numbers, time spent with friends roaming within the timelessness would be hours well spent.

The week was golden autumn sunshine on a grand scale of near-perfect dimensions. Earlier, my friends and I chased grouse in the open Crop Reserve Program land that stretches forever out here.

Either the birds or the trout would be enough by themselves, but when I happen upon both, life is sweet. Such is the situation on this trip—plenty of grouse, a few Huns, and lots of big, fat rainbows that rise aggressively to a dry fly. The end of the warm-weather feeding binge is underway. Even if these weren't almost unfished-for trout, they would be easy marks at this time of the year—a flimflam con for lazy fly fishers everywhere—as they work determinedly to pack away energy reserves for the approaching dark winter. To eat is to perhaps live to next spring. To do anything less borders on a death sentence.

One day while the others walked the fields; I romped a delightful little pond full of shifty fish only minutes from town—the angling made special by the companionship of a man who had fished the water for decades.

Caddis were rising everywhere in small, disorganized clouds, and because of the warm weather there were even a few electric blue damselflies darting across the surface in search of minute prey. Drys cast sixty or seventy feet from shore took trout on almost every cast. Twitching and skittering the patterns across the glassy water drove the big rainbows nuts, and they splashed and knifed after the imitations, creating a wonderful wet racket and providing fine sport. We took trout to four pounds. Despite the numbers, the fishing never turned boring. The day was too nice, illuminated with a subtle crystal October light that glows more than shines, throwing a surreal cast on the wide-open landscape. I released all of my fish while my friend kept a couple for dinner with his wife.

We rolled back through the wheat fields turned silver-white in the light of a rising moon. Deer browsed along the road and the lights of town sparkled in the distance. Coming down off the high plains to the gentle valley was like landing on another planet—the road was smooth and the Jeep ran quietly as we hummed along at eighty-five or so.

That evening over a little bourbon and casual talk we pretty much figured that life was awfully good out here in central Montana—good friends, a few birds, and some trout leaping around for the hell of it. We were all easy and easy to please at this point in the proceedings.

The next morning was clear, cloudless, just like the other ones as we piled into our vehicles for the three-hour drive south to Hardin, a land of distant mountain ranges and high rolling plains that float off into oblivion with gay abandon, as they say.

Out through Grassrange, on past Roundup and the burned-over Bull Mountains, quickly around the crowded oiltown madness of Billings and on into Hardin right next to the Crow Indian Reservation to fill up with gas and other necessities. Some of today's serious angling action pours in from the south on the Bighorn River just outside of town, where chasing huge trout and dodging hordes of aggressive fly fishers means big bucks in a poor land. Arid badlands and the Pryor Mountains are over this way, too.

Tomorrow we would wander over east of I90 and hunt grouse around the Little Wolf Mountains, but today we pitch extraneous gear in our motel rooms and strike off to a ranch with thousands and thousands of acres of land rolling away untouched in the shadow of the Bighorn Mountains. And that's where I first found the ranch-pond trout.

This type of fishing will never be confused with chasing native rainbows in the wild rivers of Alaska (or so I've been told) or even with that found out on the lakes of the Blackfeet Reservation.

You know that there are tons of big trout where you are going. Often the best waters are off-limits to all but a favored few, but a person can usually gain access by politely asking permission from the owner. Finding these easy-fishing, no-brainer waters is often a matter of listening to bar rumor or random sport-shop conversation. Or maybe you're one of the lucky ones who has family or friends who own a pond or two.

Whatever the case, this is the type of fly fishing that is fun a couple of times a season. Too much sours the experience, but it is perfect for adding a little spice and variety to an extended bird-hunting trip. Most of the lakes are full of freshwater shrimp or minnows or aquatic insects, which translates into astounding growth rates and huge trout. The first ten-pounder I ever caught (just one of many thousand now, of course) came at a ranch pond on the first cast. A huge rainbow that leaped once then sounded and sulked for a few minutes before I horsed the sucker in. Nothing spectacular in the way of acrobatics, but a hell of a fish all the same and my hands shook as I removed the hook and released the dark-colored creature.

Somewhere between Lodge Grass and Wyola, way back from the interstate, we pull into the ranch we are going to hunt (and perhaps fish?). The owner directs us up to a dirt road that climbs easily on top of a bench that crests for miles—tended fields, thick draws, and a pleasant little creek sliding by below (which we later learned yields a five-pound trout or two each year to those few willing to try and in the know—a local, watery legend with well-kept-secret overtones).

We get out and stretch and really take our time putting on boots, checking guns, loading shells, just kind of savoring the view and an autumn day that is special anywhere but is stone-cold magic in Montana.

Fall, and temperatures in the eighties, no wind, only a piece past noon—we all agree that our timing is right in the pocket, all right, but this is nice country and we could walk a little with our guns, couldn't we?

We work right at the edge of the bench, where the land drops

Casting for cruising rainbows on a central Montana ranch pond.

away down to that small stream of piscatorial secrets. Some air moves along here but we fail to kick up any birds. And pushing down one draw and then up part of another is hot business in less than an hour.

Consensus reigns, and the draw will be walked out and then back to the vehicle and its cheerful cooler of ice-cold beer. A real dedicated bunch on this bluebird day.

The heat and the muffled sounds of the others trudging along the steep sides of the ravine and a few flies doing a half-assed job of annoying me are a well-remembered bird-hunting rhythm that is swiftly blown away as dozens of sharps rocket out of the thick, thorny growth in the center of the draw.

There are grouse everywhere and I just manage to raise my gun and wave the barrel at the sky—the sun has hammered an infrared voodoo dullness into my eroded reflexes. But two of the others drop a pair of birds each and we retrieve these in the dying, browning tall grasses and thistle, all the while keeping a good mark on where the rest of the sharps came down.

And we fan out uphill to flush the birds again. They break in 360 degrees, busting out all over the place, forcing two of us to pass on decent shots while two others hit a pair each, the birds dropping down and away in the sky, falling through the purple-haze Bighorns shimmering on the horizon.

Another hour passes this way and finds us back at the truck cleaning the grouse, drinking the beer, and mostly talking about nothing much, which always seems to be more than enough after a good bit of now-easy work in the field.

The sun is almost gone. The air is chill. And steaks to be grilled outside wait back at the ranch house.

Tomorrow we'd strike out for the severe emptiness of those Little Wolf Mountains between town and Colstrip for some more sharptails. Hot and dry and early in the season, but the hunting is still worthwhile. Nothing new about this, either.

A full moon is making a normally dark motel parking lot look like daylight, and the time is around midnight. You do not have to be a rocket scientist to know that our luck is going to hold up under the strain of our expectations tomorrow.

The Crow and others survived here for eons well before cruisers like trappers and Custer strolled through native turf. The tribe is still around, and you see members shuffling along the dusty roads and working at gas stations here and there, in small towns like Crow Agency and Indian Arrow.

Whites are not a real popular tune on the Reservation or, for that matter, on the neighboring Northern Cheyenne Reservation, and this situation complicates our simple bird-hunting goals and dreams.

Crow tribal government is in a state of transition that may well sort itself out within a year or so, or the chaos may linger into the next century. There are three types of land holdings that concern the hunter: tribal, belonging to all Crow members; individual tribal member holdings; and private deeded land owned by non-tribal members, like the benchland we hunted yesterday.

White ranchers, guides, and outfitters, in a rare fit of unanimity, all agree that a wise individual steers well clear of tribal land, even the holdings of private members who may grant you access. There is too much emotion and anger swirling around out here toward whites and among Crow members.

A high school basketball game between two tribal schools erupted into a brawl that nearly resulted in serious injury or death to the officials a few years ago. And that involved a white man's game, not the very personal involvement the Crow have with hunting and the land.

There are many sections of deeded land, and despite the expansive nature of the Reservations, even more nontribal acreage lies out there waiting for the bird hunter.

The morning is already getting warm under the encouragement of a cloudless sky as we kick at the dirt of a small turnout just off a state highway while waiting for our guide, who pulls up in a truck and a cloud of dust.

Soon pavement gives way to dirt as we wind through rugged hills of thick sandstone capped with red clinker. Pine covers much of the hills. The truck ahead skids sideways to a halt, the two occupants hop out, run to the opposite side of the road, then point into a gully and talk eagerly about something or other.

We stop, get out, and quickly pick up on the flock of turkeys that must be fifty, sixty birds running with serious haste into forested cover. That's a lot of turkeys, and they are healthy creatures. Several more groups of similar size are spotted during the rest of the morning. Turkeys are now showing up at an alarming rate in my fishing wanderings.

Behind us, huge earth-moving equipment grinds, rattles, and rumbles. Cables from a gigantic dragline arch across the horizon. This is coal country—open-pit strip mining on a scale that is difficult to grasp, even when you stare at the evidence for hard minutes.

There's sufficient coal sitting just below the topsoil around these parts to power the country for centuries, but when the black ore is all mined, what remains? The megalomaniacal power companies claim loudly and often that the earth can be reclaimed, returned to exactly the way it used to be prior to the mining intrusion. There are plans and schematics and blueprints slammed down on tables as exhibits to prove the claims at raucous public meetings held around the state that are all show and venting of spleens but signify nothing at all in the grand money-making scheme.

To be truthful, there has been some habitat temporarily reclaimed from the colossal diggings, but much habitat has also been destroyed. Only the coming years will tell whether or not man has screwed up the fragile master plan out here.

We whip over the crest of a hill and plummet quickly downward, braking wildly onto a dirt-path situation that dies away into a trail we are to take in hot pursuit of the grouse.

World-class snake country here, and I forgot my snakeproof chaps. No big deal. Ten minutes into the hunt one of us does a lunging, lurching pirouette at the sound of a rasping, rattling buzz. The creature is blown away by the guide's twelve-gauge. He does not like snakes in the least, we learn.

A couple of hours of no grouse and only a few not-yet-the-season pheasants creates a touch of negative attitude that drifts away over lunch.

A stock pond of several acres lies just behind the open-sided barn we are eating in. The ranch owner says to "give it a shot," so I rig my battered 6-weight Orvis travel rod (I used to think it was way too stiff, now it acts a bit sloppy, as we all do on occasion as the years roll by), tie on a hopper—it's warm and the choice seems appropriate—and walk down to the water. The line unfurls over the water and the bug lands on the still surface. I wait for the small ripples to die a natural death before twitching the thing—just like bass fishing. Out of nowhere a large rainbow breaks the surface and pounces on the fly. I set the hook, and the prick of the sharp metal triggers a bouncing, tail-flapping display of anger and confusion that culminates with the high-pitched *ping* of the tippet popping from too much strain—provided by the fish and by my pressuring the rod too much.

Several more casts result in two more break-offs and one very nice trout of over twenty inches.

"Nice work, Holt. One out of four. Twenty-five percent. At least it's better than your attendance record in college."

And this guy is my friend.

Soon it is hot again out here in this land that seemed smooth and benign when glassed from the morning's ridgetop vantage.

Small puffs of alkali soil curl up around my boots before settling noiselessly onto clumps of cactus and parched grasses. More than a couple of miles of walking and no birds, and common thoughts of Why am I here? and Let's call it a day bounce among the wild forms of eroded sandstone.

Pausing to rest on a slab of rock, I see two of my companions working an overgrown curving slice in the landscape, and then I see them raise their guns and swing on targets unseen from where I sit. Guns are already being lowered when the sounds of shooting arrive.

Renewed by the excitement of this action and the prospect of some more, I quickly make my way down the bone-dry drainage in time to see several grouse stuffed into hunting-vest game pouches.

As on the bench previously, what seemed to be a land without life has suddenly changed into a setting where every draw, clump of bushes, and line of tall grass adjacent to stubbled alfalfa fields holds sharptails.

There are birds everywhere and the shooting is constant, the smell of the firing hanging on dead-still air. You push your way through the thick grass that is like knee-deep snow in January and the grouse take flight with loud wingbeats, hanging tight to the cover, dipping and swooping over, under, and around tree limbs, bushes, rotting fence posts only to pop into view, briefly flashing in the sunlight. Sudden opportunities vanish as swiftly as they appear.

And in what seems only a moment the afternoon's hunting is done.

Again, what felt like drudgery an hour ago already is shaded with burnished golden overtones that will develop and mature in the course of numerous classic regalings and retellings to friends over cognac and Honduran cigars in the lifeless cold of winter. There is a warm fire laughing in the background and the dog is not paying attention to my tale.

At the end of the day, winter looms much closer, as it does at the end of every day in the field for me, but the dread associated with the effort of battling through long months of ice and darkness is diminished some. Chasing grouse and hunting big trout predictably works this magic each autumn—an elegant example of divine vices turned necessities.

To do nothing but prepare my home for the approaching northland-storm blastings would be like hanging out on death row.

On the drive back to our rooms the sun is down and we stop in the middle of a dirt road to look one last time at the land we fished and hunted.

A huge white moon makes a stylish appearance just over the horizon. It's big but also appears small in the limitless silence. A soft touch of sage drifts on an evening breeze, and still there is no sound and there are no artificial lights anywhere.

You could disappear for a long time out in this country, looking for fish and birds.

Whitefish Range

*L*ooking north from my home, the Whitefish Range dominates the skyline. The southern fringes of these mountains are covered in pine forest, except where the Big Mountain ski area has been given carte blanche by the U.S. Forest Service to clear-cut new runs as it sees fit. Running north into Canada, the country retains a rugged, undisturbed character despite extensive timber cutting in many of the drainages. The North Fork of the Flathead River defines the eastern edge of this area. The Stillwater flowing south into Whitefish and the Tobacco River running north into Lake Koocanusa mark the western border.

As is to be expected in this part of the world, grizzlies, eagles, elk, deer, moose, wolverines, porcupines, martens, beavers, and native populations of both cutthroat and bull trout live here. Even with the intrusions of a growing population of people like me, this is still fine country. Despite its somewhat tame appearance when compared to the wild granite madness of Glacier Park, this is the type of terrain that can kill you in an instant if you are careless. Becoming disoriented (as in "lost," a state I am now quite comfortable with) is easy to do, especially way back in the dark stillness of the remaining old-growth forest.

The cutthroat are what attract my attentions from a still-water perspective. There are dozens and dozens of lakes and ponds in these hills, named and unnamed. Cutthroat swim in both varieties, although hiking in to a lake that is not even on the map has all the earmarks of a snipe hunt. Most are barren. The few that have trout one year may freeze out the following winter. A good example is a group of lakes lying about twenty miles north of town. A closed-off logging road leads the way, then a mile of bush-whacking finishes the trek. Six little ponds are spread out in a glen guarded by tall fir snags that are home to a surly population of three-toed woodpeckers. Every time I come here they start yell-ing all sorts of avian obscenities in my direction. The braver ones dive-bomb me as I sweat my way to the water. They give up after a while and watch me, silently, from barren limbs. Casting to trout with this feathered crew surveilling from above is surreal. Analo-gies to a certain movie are inescapable.

At any rate, four of the little lakes are fishless (at least for me), but the two largest at the end of the draw hold cutthroat, nice fat ones that average better than a foot. In late summer, when this population spawns up here, they are wonderfully full of color. Working out forty or fifty feet of line and letting a greased Hare's Ear float in the surface film takes fish after fish. For three years running I could count on this place. I kept the water to myself and only walked in once a year. Then Montana went through a very cold winter under a deep blanket of snow. Apparently no light reached this water, eliminating what little oxygen genera-tion there was under the ice. Two hours of casting everything from midge pupae to midge nymphs to a Griffith's Gnat (and these are all great plays on mountain lakes) were fruitless. The birds on the limbs jeered without sound. A tough bunch. I tried caddis pupae, tent-winged caddis, even Goddard Caddis, with no luck. The woodpeckers were eating this up. Woolly Worms, a damsel dry (a tie I have no faith in, but it produces for others), a Badger Matuka, and a Black-Nose Dace. I was desperate, but nothing worked, and I knew the boys looking down from above were having a high old time at my expense.

I realized that I was taking myself and my fishing a bit too seriously when I caught myself flipping off the three-toed brigade. They kept staring at me, motionless. Standing there in the middle of nowhere giving the finger to a bunch of birds, I was forced to admit that I was acting the fool, and while I was well-practiced

A Whitefish Range lake with Glacier National Park in the background.

in this behavior, a little bit of foolishness (much like bluegrass music) goes a long way. This was beautiful country shining under a beautiful sky and I was alone. The fish were frozen out. Long gone. Dead. So what? Take the game as it comes. Don't sweat the small stuff and try to get everyone naked is sage advice a friend once gave me. I looked at the birds in the trees. I didn't think so. Wisdom to be sure, but not with this group.

One aspect of lake fishing that intrigues me and provides a healthy balance to river action is that in still water it is the trout that are moving and not the water. Just the opposite holds true in streams. Obviously this thought is not a new one, but it offers succinct tactical advice for me when I'm working small mountain lakes. When fish are not rising, it's more than likely they are cruising, unless the water is excessively warmed from summer's heat. If I fail to turn a trout with either drys or a few nymphs, I switch to the gaudiest streamer I own, or at least a Zonker. A bit of probing around the shore and out in the middle (this can be futile on big water) often reveals where the trout are holding. Often the streamer even takes fish—large ones. This is fly fishing's equivalent of a fish locator and has saved an outing more than once for me. With cutthroat the method is excellent. They are rarely fished over in their wild hangouts. Spooky they are not. Browns, rainbows, and to a lesser extent brookies are sometimes put off by this behavior, forcing me to rest the water. Cigars come in handy at times like these.

Then there are the days when you come in over the ridge and see a lake surface boiling with rising fish. The Whitefish Range and a number of its lakes have given me this rush many times. Jamming the rod together, tearing line through the guides, and tying on something sophisticated (like a Royal Humpy), I crash madly through the brush, banging knees and shins on deadfalls, stumps, and sleeping deer. Following recovery from a delicate pancake approach at the lake's shore, I make my first accurate offerings. After about ten minutes of untangling leader and flies from nearby spruce trees, I've usually settled down to the point where actually throwing some line on the water is a realistic possibility. The trout are still feeding like mad (they *are* cutthroats, after all) and one immediately sips my fly. The fish thrashes about and comes meekly to shore. Not energetic battlers, but they are native and they are wild and they are a sight: black spots, red-orange cuts, and golden bellies. A firm, healthy fish. Releasing this one is harder than turning loose a five-pound brown. There is something powerful, special about cutthroats, even at this little lake surrounded by mountains pockmarked with clear-cuts. The land is still feral, but God, what it must have been like one hundred years ago. I wish I could have seen this water when it was surrounded by a forest of fir and larch that was centuries, not decades, old. I'd gladly walk the twenty miles in here. You can have the damn logging roads. Give me an escape route. A chance to disappear.

But I do have the logging roads and there are times when the accessibility they offer is welcome (this is probably the first nice thing in print I have ever said about logging, even though several gypo (private) loggers are friends. They have an awareness and concern for the woods).

One road leads to a small lake within thirty minutes of home and it is full of cutthroat trout. Float tubes work here, but I prefer to use a little one-man canoe. Sitting in the wicker seat gliding around the tranquil pond casting periodically to feeding fish has a patrician quality that I find reassuring and the least bit deserved (I can justify anything given enough time). The disadvantage to the ease afforded by logging roads is that a hell of a lot of other anglers put them to the same use. Tiny lakes are either fished out or their trout populations traumatized within the first few weeks of the season. Afterward the waters are not worth fishing until early October, when most individuals are out hunting.

A bizarre example of this roadside availability happened to me one summer a few years ago. I motored my way up to a beautiful little lake lying below a mountain of shattered rock and severe avalanche chutes. There is a primitive campground here, but during the middle of the week the place is often in the deserted mode. Not this time. A large motor home from Florida (no, not my parents, but speaking of requiring adult supervision . . . but that's another story) was parked near the water, bright blue-and-white striped awning extended. Lawn furniture unfolded. Cool drinks displayed on an aluminum camp table. An inviting scene, but where were the people? I rigged up a 2-weight and worked around the shore through some battered pines and scrub under-growth to a place where fractured boulders protruded from the lake's surface. There are always nice cutthroat trout here. The Adams floated sedately on the water. I watched as a trout drifted up from cover and inhaled the fly. The fish splashed and tugged and then was released. This continued for some time until it dawned on me that there was music in the air. Was I dead and in heaven? I didn't think so.

I climbed up on a rocky point and looked around. Back at the motor home, about a hundred yards from me across the lake, a silver-haired woman was seated at an organ, playing away with abandon, her body weaving with the music. They must have dragged the thing outside while I was playing with the trout. Her mate (I assume) was reclining in a chaise nearby sipping a tall cool one. The musician finished up "Some Enchanted Evening," and then broke into a lively rendition of "Cocktails For Two."

That was all for me. I hoofed it swiftly back to the truck, tossed my gear in back, and drove the hell out of there. I've had enough weirdness in my life that I don't feel I have to endure "Cocktails For Two" at seventy-two-hundred feet above sea level in northwest Montana. Man, I knew Florida was twisted. I'd been there before, but this was too much for me at this stage in my life. Hitting Highway 93, I turned north toward the Point Of Rocks Bar where I downed an Anchor Steam Ale. Fishing. Organ music. Motor homes. Sanity.

There is another lake and I'll name the poor thing—Weasel. This used to be a beautiful little gem filled with native westslope cutthroat. Forest and mountains provided the natural backdrop. A small creek dropped away down a narrow gorge. A nice place to camp for a night or two and catch a few trout. Not any more. For some reason, one or more government agencies decided that this would be a perfect lake for bait fishers. The last time I saw the place, boardwalks were built all over the place, including a charming bridge over the creek. Several wooden platforms looking for all the world like decks in need of hot tubs jutted out over the water. A dozen people were casting spoons, drowning worms, and tossing canned corn at a population of very small hatchery trout: skinny, sickly, tin-colored things. Everyone was laughing and shouting and bumming beer and cigarettes from one another. I'm glad that a good time was being had by all, but why trash a pristine lake in the process? I don't get the picture.

Not far from Weasel and back to the southwest lies a drainage that is prime grizzly country. Bears are everywhere, thankfully. Hiking up to the lake that is the stream's headwaters is an energizing experience. Bear sign is all over the place. Scat. Tracks. Torn up logs. Fur.

From the road above one July day I watched as a sow griz and her two cubs frolicked in this creek. Mom rolled around in the cool flow and the kids were just kids, racing back and forth and up into the trees playing tag. I took all this in for over an hour and the vision is as clear (if not clearer) today than when I first viewed the spectacle. The lake takes a few hours to reach and it is located in a cirque that "looks like the moon" to fisheries biologist Tom Weaver, and he is probably right. I've never been to the moon that I know of, but I bet the landscape is similar. Gray-and-white rock. Treeless. Blasted clean by the elements (I know — no atmosphere, so no weather, on the moon). Empty. The one major difference in this drainage is the lake, blue-green and deep and filled with cutthroat.

This is an interesting place to enter and fish, especially if you spend the night. Bear vibes really wail up here, but I have never seen a grizzly in this spot. Down below among the stream, yes, but fortunately not at the lake. Knowing they are present, padding softly through the trees just out of my sight or hearing is more than enough. Their absence would destroy for me the joy of traveling this country.

The fishing is almost an afterthought. So damn far away from all of the societal crap, hanging out in this rocky landscape above treeline is a relief. The mountains of western Glacier to the east are radiant in the sunset. The lake's surface is now green-black with silver light sparkling off the rise rings of the feeding cutthroat. I shoot one long cast out toward the heart of the water and a big fish takes right away. Strong, it takes line from the reel and the drag sounds surprised. Cutthroat do not normally fight this hard. More line gone, then the trout boils far from me. It's large, with an impressive dorsal. Slowly it comes to me. Its length is stunning — approaching twenty inches, black-backed and spotted, crimson flashes on the lower jaw and along the belly with shades of copper and gold.

A damn good fish.

But then, this is damn good country.

Northern Rockies Beaver Ponds

*T*he time was past for chasing brook trout in this pond. The fish were already on their redds, spawning colors intense even when viewed through the distance of several feet of water. Hundreds of trout from eight inches to more than twenty were holding on large patches of clean gravel scattered about this shallow shelf that resembled saltwater flats I'd seen long ago in Florida.

Under an overcast late-October sky the canoe glided softly across the glassy water. Pairs of fish were wrapping tails and fins around each other, depositing eggs and milt. The size of some of these trout was astounding. They never moved from the beds. The sight of the canoe overhead held no fear or interest for them. Earlier, out of curiosity and an overwhelming predatory need, I'd cast a large Zonker over a spawning area. I had clipped the hook off at the shank. I only wanted to move a fish, to see how aggressive the trout were. The streamer landed well beyond the holding brookies and sank to the bottom. I began dragging it along the bottom. Before the fly reached the redd a pack of trout charged. The largest fish banged the thing with its nose, then tried to swallow it. I jerked the Zonker toward me, but the trout held on briefly, sending a strong message back up along the line before it released its prey. Another cast produced similar results and I called a halt to my greed. Prior to paddling out on this water, I walked through a stand of old cottonwoods and peered around

131

the trunk of one tree and looked into a creek running down the hills toward the pond, not more than three or four feet wide with small pockets of holding water. Each miniature hole held brook trout. Fish of a foot, maybe a bit longer, stacked up in the current. When I stepped out from behind the tree, the trout scattered for shelter beneath the banks and under clumps of exposed roots. Spawning was in high gear.

Two weeks earlier I'd caught a number of brook trout here as they raced about in the embryonic throes of breeding frenzy. But now, at this time in the cycle, the fishing was way too easy. Every cast would take a good trout. The fish did not need my intrusion. Stress and injury from my attentions might damage them. So I just floated around the pond taking in the sights, content to know I could always return to fish and watch next season. To have something like this so close to home is special. This is an event I wait for each autumn. It's a part of my yearly routine, like seeking out rainbows in the spring or hunting sharp-tailed grouse in late September.

Beaver ponds offer a different form of still-water angling. Brook trout are not native to Montana and they often drive out native cutthroat or crossbreed with bull trout. In such cases they are more than a nuisance, but in many spots they offer fine sport. The best of these ponds, like the one near my home, are full of trout, usually brookies, though rainbows, cutthroats, and even browns take up residence in these somewhat artificial environments. Despite the numbers of fish they contain, they are difficult to figure out and the action is inconsistent. In warmer weather my favorites are studies in frustration. Trout will be rising to emergers, then duns, and finally spinners. Occasionally I match what is happening and fool a few of them. More commonly, the fish ignore my efforts and take something else nearby. In desperation I've worked through my patterns imitating *Callibaetis,* caddis, Tricos, *Hexagenia,* and on into the realms of sow bugs, waterboatmen, and finally large streamers—without result. Sink-Tips in the middle of a beaver pond. Drys and nymphs in the fertile littoral zone along shore. Nothing. I've chased the hatches from the early stages of the warmer water of the shallows out gradually deeper along thick weed beds. I've dredged submerged stream channels running darkly along the bottom. Still nothing.

Time and study are needed to learn the well-defined rhythms of these places. One pond I know is filled with fish, but until the sun slides down behind the trees and deep shadows creep out over the water, nothing happens. The water seems devoid of trout. But from that magic moment on, the surface is alive with working brook trout and a direct match is required. Often, caddis, midges, and mayflies are hatching simultaneously. I have enough trouble figuring things out when they appear singly and are straightforward in behavior. Add a couple of species to the mix and mayhem runs riot in my fly selection. Drys from #10 to #24, blanketing the spectrum of aquatic insects existing in Montana, are hastily tied on, cast to the trout, and then snipped off. My tippet does a vanishing act from 7X to 2X in minutes. Convincing myself that a #20 Pale Evening Dun looks like its natural counterpart floating on its head while attached to something resembling an anchor rope is an act of faith that transcends belief in the legitimacy of the Shroud of Turin.

Out of frustration I've actually rebuilt my leader and tied on an Elk-Wing Caddis and skittered the thing across the water in a clumsy imitation of the natural. This approach takes trout, for a time, then the commotion of the retrieve stops the feeding in a circle of one hundred yards or so. I sit and wait for the rising to start once again, and when I see the brookies dimpling the water I try my one-trick approach, but the fish are hip to the con and ignore the fly. A mayfly spinner (the methodical approach to the dilemma in full swing here) is tied on and tossed out. Eventually, near the end of the feeding binge a trout or two takes the fly, but sitting and watching while all hell is breaking loose around me is maddening. I'd rather work a nymph or swim a streamer, even if this scares off the fish.

There are hundreds (thousands?) of beaver ponds in the Rockies. Beavers have made a full-scale comeback from their earlier population decline, and their dams, diversions, and riparian harvestings of trees and bushes are a common sight. These ponds are a compression of lake fishing for me. Most of the impoundments are only a few surface acres. The water is exceptionally clear and the brook trout can see everything. There is not a lot of habitat to probe and explore. Do everything right and very quietly and a fish *might* be tricked. The myth that beaver ponds are easy pickings is just that, a myth. Water that is rarely worked will yield a quick trout, but they soon spook and then I must analyze the situation. Not my strong point. Nor is delicate casting. Ask my friends.

Floating a pond after sunset in a tube has yielded some large fish, but paddling about in total darkness creates elements of barely restrained fear in me. The chances of being dragged under by a five-pound brook trout are slim. All the same, I cannot help but wonder about my dangling legs. Plopping a large dry fly like a #8 Adams on the surface surrounded by the sounds of trout feeding is interesting. Ripples from the movements of what must be very big fish bump against the tube. When a brookie takes the fly and the rod tip is pulled suddenly down into the water, the game is on. A sense of size is gleaned from the intensity of the struggle. Break-offs are frequent. I never know exactly where I or the fish are on the water in the night. Bringing a trout of several pounds to net and taking my first glimpse of it in the dim yellow beam of a penlight is always a wonder.

Catching these guys turns loose the adrenalin, but I'm relieved when I finally reach shore and step out of the water. There is nothing to fear, but being on the water in the dark scares me anyway, like looking over the edge of a high dam in spite of my acrophobia. Challenging my fears occasionally is worthwhile, but I do not have an ice-climber's addiction to terror. Once or twice a year alone on a lake at night is sufficient.

One of the pure joys of beaver ponds is that you never know where you will find one. A stream that you have not visited in a couple of years may now have a dam and an acre of water behind it. Sure, some quality runs may have been destroyed, but the sight of smooth water covered with riseforms is reasonable compensation.

A beautiful beaver-pond brook trout in full spawning regalia.

As you creep to the edge of the pile of sticks, green alder branches, and woven grasses, the water feels cold spurting through leaks in the structure. I peer cautiously over the dam. Good fish are working right above me. Carefully, pulling out coils of line and then lightly shooting a cast onto the pond is nerve-wracking in the best way. The fly lands softly and the trout keep feeding. One sips in an insect and then another coming steadily closer. I hold motionless and watch the torpedo shape come toward the Adams. The fish pauses below and then takes. The brook trout runs with the set of the hook, and the struggle on a light rod is a balanced one—the fifteen-inch fish and the six-foot rod. The equipment and I win this round. Standing up to reach over the dam for the fish scares away the others.

This does not matter. One good trout from a pond I never knew existed is plenty. Next time on this creek I can try and catch another.

Conclusion:
Real Compared To What?

In a year devoted to fishing lakes, ponds, and reservoirs, casting to large working rainbows on a piece of isolated water close to home on Halloween seems appropriate.

After chasing the noble goldfish (or Koi as they are more accurately called, I'm told) in southeast Montana or seeking big trout out on the plains or wild cutthroats in the mountains with a background of strained organ music, finishing out the still-water year on October 31 has a nice sense of closure.

The water is cold. I can feel the hypothermic dimensions of the chill through my clothes and waders. The fish are moving about with an intentness that speaks to the approaching winter. A storm is rolling in over the western skyline. Snow dusts the trees above me.

Moving water attracted most of my attentions up until a few years ago. Now lakes and streams hold equal interest. There is an excitement that comes from watching a big trout cruising near shore, that barely perceptible rise in a lake's surface as the fish feeds confidently. False-casting and then launching a nymph toward the unseen target hoping that the fly is drifting through the creature's line of vision is charged with anticipation. When the line makes a slight move away from me in the float tube and I set the hook, the first feelings of resistance from the surprised trout are a tonic. All thoughts of everyday silliness vanish.

Focus narrows perfectly to just the fish and me. Nothing else matters. The stillness of a pond adds to this sensation in a way

136

that a river cannot. Moving water has well-defined parameters of bankside branches, strong current, plunge pools, and the like. The open playing field of a lake reduces the struggle to the basics. There is often more than enough room to play the game to a conclusion. The only questions, and they are more than enough, are: Will the trout snap the tippet? Will the hook straighten? Will my haphazardly tied clinch knot hold?

Bobbing around a lake holding on for dear life while a rainbow runs and then tail-walks across the surface has crazy overtones. The fish jumps above me. The only sound is that of disturbed water. The silent audience of larch turning gold or maybe a group of deer holding in the forest is at once spectacular, humbling, lonely, magic.

Montana's rivers are enough for any of us. To add the wonder of lakes is a blessing and I am grateful. This, along with my family, friends, and writing, are all I could ask for. All I need.

The snow squall moves overhead, throwing wet snow on the water. My fingers are frozen and I head back to shore. I have had plenty this season. That is, until a fish hits my nymph. I keep on my course and the trout fights in the opposite direction as large hail begins banging on my head and bouncing off the float tube. Twenty feet away the rainbow leaps and is nailed by a hailstone. I hear the dull "thwack."

Knocked cold, the trout lies in the water. I pull the stunned fish to me. Its dull eyes look up as I release the hook and try and revive it. Life comes fluttering back through the rainbow's body and the strangest thing happens: I can sense what the trout is thinking. The image is a dead clear flash of insight.

The message is, "Man, nobody told me about things like this happening way out in the woods."

The rainbow pulls away from my hands, racing for cover and I think, I know what you mean, buddy. I really know.

Notes and Comment

Fishing lakes in Montana differs in many respects from working rivers. One of the biggest variations is that there are not as many knowledgeable guides and outfitters willing to work still waters. Most of the heat, pressure, interest, and fame buzzes around the state's rivers. The few mentioned here will put you on to fish, even under trying weather conditions. There are others, but I have either never fished with them or know little or nothing about their reputations or abilities.

As I mentioned in my book *Knee Deep in Montana's Trout Streams,* much of the excitement associated with any fishing trip revolves around planning the adventure. The following is a brief listing of guides, outfitters, and related sources of information to help you on your merry way.

Montana in General

The state of Montana has a high-quality tourism promotion department called Travel Montana (800-541-1447 for out of state calls and 444-2654 inside the state) that publishes a couple of excellent booklets that will point travelers in many appropriate directions. They are titled *Montana Recreation Guide* and *Montana Lodging Guide,* and there is also a state highway map. There is enough information in these publications concerning guides, outfitters, hotels, motels, and campgrounds to set up a fishing excursion anywhere in the state.

As for clothing, even in August there can be snow in higher elevations. So pack for spring, summer, and fall weather, including rain gear. I always stuff a spare pair or two of wool socks, a knit hat, and some fingerless mittens in the back of my vest for those sudden spates of cold and wet nastiness that the northern Rockies are justly famous for. I keep all of this in a zip-lock bag. (Sometimes a pair of dry socks can be utter bliss.)

There is an abundance of foul-weather gear on the market, but the best all-purpose coat I have ever used (for wind, rain, cold, sleet, and the rest of the crud hanging around out there) is the Barbour Smock. It is warm, wind- and moisture-resistant, and has large pockets with room to carry plenty of gear. Although it's expensive, almost three hundred dollars, it has enabled me to fish in truly ugly conditions. Good sunglasses, hat, insect repellent, and hiking boots are necessities.

In times of little or no wind I use an Orvis HLS Adams 4-weight with a Cortland 444 Floating Nymph-Tip fly line mounted on an Abel #0 reel. The line has a red strike indicator that is ideal for detecting subtle takes, especially in tough light conditions. The setup is admittedly expensive, but even derelict writers deserve a few fine toys.

On larger waters or when the wind kicks up or when I am using a sinking tip line, I favor a Loomis IMX nine-foot 6-weight with a 7-weight line (the rod casts superbly with the heavier line). For sinking tip lines I use Teeny nymph lines. They are the best. Period.

During hurricane conditions, such as those found on the Blackfeet Reservation, the Orvis HLS Powerhouse 8-weight allows me to rocket out eighteen-foot casts with ease, even into the teeth of the gale. When the wind blows, all you can do is do the best you can.

Bring chest waders (neoprene, and lightweights for warm days and water temperatures). Hippers limit your wading range. A good float tube and fins are also nice for covering more water than you can from shore.

Licenses cost less than fifty dollars per season, and it's ten dollars for two days for nonresidents. Most waters are open all year if you like ice fishing. Some (but not enough) are catch-and-release only. Pick up a copy of the *Montana Fishing Regulations* when you purchase your license. Current information is available from the Montana Department of Fish, Wildlife and Parks, 1420 East Sixth Avenue, Helena 59620; (406) 444-2535.

Tongue Reservoir, Central Montana Ponds

You're pretty much on your own out in the flatland wilds of the state. Everyone I've met traveling back here has been friendly and helpful. Always try and find the landowner and ask permission (this is good advice for any private water in Montana) before making a cast.

Beartooth Mountains

Beartooth Plateau Outfitters, operated by Ronnie L. Wright: Box 1127, Main Street, Cooke City 59020; June–September (406) 838-2328, October–May (406) 445-2293.

Fort Peck Reservoir

Jordan Chamber of Commerce, Jordan 59337; (406) 557-2480.

Merrell Lake

Hubbard's Yellowstone Lodge, Box 662, Emigrant 59027; (406) 848-7755. From December 15 through April 15: 5300 Gulf Drive, Holmes Beach, Florida 34217; (813) 778-7028.

Sweetgrass Hills

Shelby Chamber of Commerce, Box 865, Shelby 59474; (406) 434-7184.

Flathead Lake, Whitefish Range
Northwest Lakes, Grayling Lakes
Northern Rockies Beaver Ponds

Lakestream Fly Fishers is run by George Widener, who has a serious interest in fishing the unique and offbeat waters and species, along with preserving same. An excellent guide for northwest Montana. 15 Central Avenue, Whitefish 59901; (406) 862-1298.

Grouse Mountain Lodge (1205 Highway 98 West, Whitefish 59937; (800) 321-8822 or 862-3000 in state) has rooms starting at $77, along with a restaurant and lounge. The Whitefish Lake Restaurant (862-5285) just across the highway has good food.

Flathead National Forest office, 1935 Third Avenue East, Kalispell 59901; (406) 755-5401, has maps of the country. Whitefish Chamber of Commerce, 525 East Third Street, Whitefish 59937; (406) 862-3501.

Hidden Lake

Glacier National Park, West Glacier 59936; (406) 888-5441.

Lake X

Joe Kipp knows the fishing on the Blackfeet Reservation as well as anyone. Morning Star Outfitters, Box 968, Browning 59417; (406) 338-2785.

Tribal licenses cost $7.50 per day, $15 for three days, and $35 for the season. A license for a float tube is currently $5. All of these prices will probably rise on an almost yearly basis. A Montana license is also required.

The War Bonnet Lodge has rooms for around $40 per night, along with a cafe: Jct. 2 and Hwy 89, Browning 59417; (406) 338-7610. The Summit Station Restaurant and Lounge has fine food and is located about ten minutes west of East Glacier: (406) 226-4428.

Blackfeet Tribal Offices, call (406) 338-7806 for further travel information.

Georgetown Lake

Catch Montana is run by John Adza: Box 428, Hamilton 59840; (800) 882-7844. You can stay at The Lodge and then drive over the beautiful Skalkaho Pass for the day's fishing. Owner John Talia has designed one of the sweetest lodges in the west along the banks of the Bitterroot River.

Bitterroot Valley Chamber of Commerce, 105 East Main Street, Hamilton 59840; (406) 363-6078.

Clark Canyon Reservoir

Tim Tollett, Frontier Anglers, Box 11, Dillon 59725; (800) 228-5263. The Bannack House is the restaurant of choice in the area: 33 East Bannack, Dillon 59725; (406) 683-5088.

Beaverhead County Chamber of Commerce, Box 830, Dillon 59725; (406) 683-5511.

Kicking Horse Reservoir

Natural Resources Department of Confederated Salish and Kootenai Tribes, Box 278, Pablo 59855; (406) 675-2700.

Ronan Chamber of Commerce, Box 254, Ronan 59864; (406) 676-8300.

Further Reading

The Complete Book of Western Hatches, by Rick Hafele and Dave Hughes, contains some good information on the major species in Montana. Frank Amato Publications, 1981.

Flyfishing the High Country, by John Gierach, offers chapters on high-country lakes and beaver ponds. Pruett Publishing Company, 1984.

Hiker's Guide to Glacier National Park, Glacier Natural History Association, 1978.

Lake Fishing With a Fly, by Ron Cordes and Randall Kaufmann, gives detailed information on lake dynamics, tactics, and fly patterns. Frank Amato Publications, 1984.

McClane's New Standard Fishing Encyclopedia, edited by A. J. McClane, contains a little bit on just about everything associated with fishing. Holt, Rinehart and Winston, 1974.

Roadside Geology of Montana, by David Alt and Donald W. Hyndman, gives the average bozo a pretty fair idea of what formed the landscape in Montana. Mountain Press Publishing Company, 1986.

Slade's Glacier, by Robert F. Jones, is a book that has absolutely nothing to do with fishing in Montana but makes fine reading during the heat-of-the-day-sipping-a-cold-one doldrums. Dell Publishing Company, 1981.

Stillwater Trout, edited by John Merwin, is an excellent technical discussion of lake fishing with a good section on fly patterns. Nick Lyons Books, 1977.

Index